THE POWER OF YOUTH
IT ALL BEGINS WITH YOU!

CARLOS OJEDA JR.

D1113958

COOLSPEAK PUBLISHING COMPANY

DEDICATION

This is dedicated to my sons, Alberto and Alesandro.
Thank you for showing me the true depth of love, for being so
fearless in how you approach life and for inspiring me to look at
the world through your eyes: in hope, awe and wonder.

Youth + POWER = CHANGE

By philosophical definition, power is the ability to influence the behavior of others with or without resistance. By our definition, power is the ability to get things done! The ability to bring about positive change in the world. True power is evident in education, technological advancement, and in revolution, but no more so than in the hands of the youth that make these things happen.

TABLE OF CONTENTS

FOREWORD By Dr. Juan Andrade

From the first time I heard Carlos as the keynote speaker at our student leadership conference almost 10 years ago in Newark, New Jersey, I knew I was hearing someone unique; someone in a league of his own. As a person who has had the opportunity to meet and hear some of the greatest voices in America over the last four decades including U.S. presidents, senators, male and female members of congress, ambassadors, governors, ministers, and motivational speakers, within minutes of hearing Carlos speak I knew that I was hearing a speaker who could summon and apply the power to change the world.

I was initially struck by his age – probably early 20s. Frankly I wasn't expecting much. Normally it takes years of experience and numerous speeches to really "find your voice", learn how to engage the audience, find the comfort level needed to deliver effectively, and many of the other qualities and skills necessary to be an effective public speaker.

Carlos totally blew me away! He clearly possessed and radiated qualities and skills far beyond anyone could reasonably expect from such a young speaker. In short, his stage presence was powerful.

The "power" was everywhere. And if there's anyone who doesn't believe that power is important, let me lovingly remind you that the Bible mentions "power" more often than it mentions "salvation".

There was power in his voice. And by that I don't mean loud. His tone was smooth; easy to listen to. The range in his voice rose and dropped effortlessly from exhilaration to sadness, triggering the intended emotional responses from the 200 high school and college students in the audience. The power in his voice stirred emotions, which I found incredibly amazing.

There was power in the authority I could hear in his voice. He knew exactly what he wanted to say, when to say it, and how to say it, which made him believable. One can speak with authority without being believable as heads of state do all the time. The power in Carlos' voice rested on the authority with which he spoke.

There was power in his message. The essence of his speech was based on his personal life experiences, which were shared in such intimate fashion that every person in the room could see themselves being at his side every step of the way.

Students could see themselves riding a bike along his side on the same sidewalk near his childhood home where he witnessed a murder, being wrongly placed in the same bilingual classroom with him in Reading, Pennsylvania.

You could see yourself going along with him to the principal's office with his Dad that didn't go the way he had expected, goofing off at school with him, and so on.

There was power in the confidence with which he shared the times in his life that he faced challenges, both successfully and unsuccessfully. He spoke candidly about being irresponsible, the consequences, and how he turned things around. There was confidence in the way he took control of his circumstances and didn't allow himself to become a victim to those circumstances, despite having created them himself.

Deeply embedded in his message was the power of hope. One can only imagine the sense of fear, self-doubt, insecurity, and despair that haunts our youth on a daily basis. Carlos' message of hope was exactly what our students needed that day, and the response that followed the conclusion of his remarks was nothing short of an altar call. Students openly cheered through their tears knowing that someone had literally spoken to the silence that had filled their hearts and their lives. They had been reluctant to dream. They had been reluctant to verbalize their hope. They had been reluctant to face their fears. They had been reluctant to confront their self-doubt. But not anymore. Carlos had in a single speech wiped their slate clean, and I witnessed the transformation of 200 students who felt inspired and armed to change the world; their world.

Perhaps what was most powerful then, as it is today, is his ability to instill in his audience the same power of hope that had transformed his own life and put him on the course of an extraordinary career.

So compelling is his story that I knew from the very first time I heard Carlos that he had a unique power to empower others; that through the power to his voice, message, and skillful delivery he could transform lives and change worlds. Over the years I have heard Carlos speak to tens of thousands of children, youth, young adults, professionals, parents and grandparents and through it all and in all of them I have witnessed his incredible power to connect, relate, motivate, empower, and transform.

In Spanish we say that "cada cabeza es un mundo"; that every head is a world. When I say that Carlos has the ability to change the world, I know it's true because he first changed his own. When he talks about others having the power to change the world; it's personal. He's talking about people having the power to change their own world first and then the world of others. Every head is its own world. Whatever a person is or could be resides in his or her own head. When you come in contact with Carlos' world, you're going to change, and change for the better. That's the power of his being. That's the power that he shares generously with those who have the opportunity, and good fortune, to hear him speak.

Carlos is an extraordinarily gifted and talented young man. He has the power to make others believe in themselves and summon the power to control their own destiny. The beauty of his power is that it serves to empower those who haven't yet discovered or summoned the strength of their own power into their lives. Hopefully through this book they will have the opportunity to see the beauty of Carlos' power at work in his own life and in the life of others, and fill every reader with the power of hope.

Dr. Juan Andrade Jr. is President of the United States Hispanic Leadership Institute, which does political organizing, research and nonpartisan voter registration and leadership development. He is a Presidential Medal recipient, honored by President Bill Clinton for "the performance of exemplary deeds of service for the nation." Under his leadership the Institute has trained over 200,000 present & future leaders, registered over two million new voters and published 425 studies on Hispanic demographics since 1982. He has worked and participated in the democratization of Mexico, Guatemala, Nicaragua, Panama, Colombia, Paraguay, Bolivia, Guyana, Suriname and Haiti. He has been recognized three times as one of the 100 most influential Hispanics in America. He has earned five college degrees, including a doctorate from Northern Illinois University and a post-doctorate M.A. from Loyola University in Chicago.

"You can not deny the lucid fact that silence must always succumb to voice." – Joaquin Zihuatanejo

YOUR VOICE IS YOUR POWER

The question mark is far more powerful than the period.

What does that mean? We'll get into that in a moment, but first, I want you to let that statement sink in.

My name is Carlos Ojeda, Jr. and I want to help you find the power that is within you. I'm not talking about some mystical inner being or The Force; I'm talking about the power that can change the world.

While your mind is wandering, wondering what could be so amazing, so immensely powerful that could change the world, it's important that you understand what the word 'world' actually means. When people talk about changing the world, they tend to think about the seven billion people, lives and cultures that they will never meet. But the 'world' is much larger than that. And much smaller.

The 'world' begins and ends with you. When you change yourself, when you take charge and find the power to change yourself and the circumstances in which you live, you begin to change the world around you.

But I'm just one person, I'm just a kid, you might be thinking.

Really?

That's the thinking that has helped us lose our power, the thinking that has led to an entire generation of young people feeling as though they have no impact on the world around them, the thinking that regardless of what you may want, it's up to *someone else* to decide whether you can have it or not.

Power is the engine of change and when you don't feel as though you have any real power, then you will certainly believe you cannot change anything, much less the world. But what if you *could* affect real change in your life? You have friends, family, and other people who listen to you.

Imagine making a change that inspires two people you know to also want to change. Then they influence two other people each. Before you know it, that simple individual has impacted hundreds of people and the engine begins powering on. So how do we get to that moment? How do we realize the hope, desire and ambition that are locked away inside of us?

The question mark is far more powerful than the period.

Okay, I'm going to explain that in a minute, but first let me tell you a little story. Maybe you'll see yourself in this story, or maybe you'll know someone who has lived this story as well. Maybe they're living it right now.

Growing up in Newark, New Jersey, in the shadows of the New York City skyline, the world around me was the only world I knew. I was the child of immigrants living in what might well have been Puerto Rico itself because everyone around me was the same. We spoke the same language, we listened to the same music, and ate the same foods. I knew *only* what I saw and heard every day.

I knew nothing of other people, different languages, other cultures; I knew nothing of anything outside my world. It was all I knew because that was all my environment taught me. When you grow up, you only learn what your environment teaches you, and you can't be blamed for that. But you can be blamed for letting it stay that way. Because the world changes and you have to change with it. When I was 10, my life changed forever.

My father was tough, but he worked hard to provide for us. Together, my mother and father set up strict rules for me to follow. I didn't understand them and I didn't question them. I merely followed them.

The question mark is far more powerful than the period.

Well, I owned a yellow bike that I could ride from my house to the corner and back. That was it. Why? I didn't know. I just knew that if I went too far, I'd hear my father's voice echo around the world.

One day I made it to the corner and watched something I will never shake. A drug deal was going down. Sure, Newark was becoming one of the most dangerous cities in America, but it was still the only world I knew. This was home. This was normal. But what happened next was anything but normal.

I watched one man pull out a gun and shoot another guy. My friends and I all scattered, running back home. I dragged that bike with me, my legs wouldn't listen and I struggled to keep up with them as they sprinted away from the scene. I mean it didn't matter if the world was falling apart, that bike had to make it home with me or my mother would let me have it.

As the cops began canvassing the area and asking questions, my father took one look at me and said, 'You didn't see anything.' Okay.

My mother took one look at him and said, 'we have to leave. We're not raising our children in this mess.' My father looked at her and all he could say was, 'Okay.'

We packed up all of our worldly possessions, which weren't too many, and left the view of New York City and landed a million miles away in a place called Reading, Pennsylvania. When I say 'a million miles away,' it was only a couple hundred in reality, but there were horses and buggies and fields and seemed to be as far from the City as you could get. I hated it.

Then came school. Talk about a brand new experience. My father went off to work so my mother, who immigrated to this country later in life and spoke English with an accent, enrolled me. They took one look at her, then me, and decided I belonged in the bi-lingual class.

Well, I think it's important to say that I spoke fluent English and Spanish, read in English and Spanish, and wrote in English and Spanish. I even *dreamed* in English and Spanish, but we won't get into any of that at this time. I sat down among a Korean, a German, and a Jamaican. All boys and nobody could understand each other. I could see this cute girl across the hall and I said I wanted to be in that class and my new teacher simply patted me on the head and said in a long, drawling voice, 'You're so cute. You stay here.'

It was three weeks before I finally said anything to my parents. After all, I thought I deserved to be in that bi-lingual class. Why?

I *didn't ask questions.* Remember, the question mark is *far more powerful* than the period.

My father heard this and the next day he went with me to school. Now, my father grew up in the city and spoke fluent English. He marched into that school with me strutting alongside thinking, 'Now you're gonna get it,' to all the teachers and staff we passed. We strolled into the office and my father, in fluent English, asked the teachers and staff to test me and place me in the right class.

They tested me. And I passed with flying colors. And I got to go to that class with the cute girl. And we strolled out of school that day, me and my father, and I was feeling like the king of the world. That is, until he smacked me upside the head so hard I had tears in my eyes.

All I could do was stare up at him.

"What was that for?" I said, timidly. "I didn't do nothing."

"Exactly," was his response. "You did nothing."

What he said next changed the course of my life forever …

"You let them put you in a corner where you didn't belong."

I tried to say something, to defend myself, but my father continued.

"You were there for three weeks. You didn't say anything. I don't send you to school to waste time. I send you to school to learn. Your voice is your power. Use it."

Your voice is your power.

"It's the one thing God gave you, so you can claim your destiny, speak your mind, stand your ground and you let them take that from you."

Your voice is your power and the question mark is far more powerful than the period. That's what you use your voice for. With that voice you ask questions. Questions get you answers. Answers give you knowledge. Knowledge gives you power. The power to change your life and the life of those around you ..."

The power to change the world.

The problem that most young people today feel is that they have no power, no voice. You feel silenced. You feel isolated, propped in a corner. You feel as though you're in the wrong classroom but no one's listening to you. But are you asking questions?

Why am I here? What does this mean? What do *I* want in life?

These are just a few questions, but they start opening more doorways to more questions and the more questions you ask, the more *knowledge* you attain and the more knowledge you have, the more *power* you *earn*.

Power isn't about beating someone up or taking what you want. Power is about making a better life for yourself and those around you. When you sit in the corner and just accept it because someone who *seemed* to know what they were doing put you there, then you have no power to change your life.

Let me pose a question to you: if you woke up tomorrow and were suddenly 30 years old, and you were living the same exact life then as you are now, would you be okay with it? Would that be good enough?

I'm betting most of you are shaking your heads right now reading that and thinking, 'No way.' You want more. You *deserve* more. Men and women throughout history have changed the world, and their own private worlds, through their own personal power. Cesar Chavez and Dolores Huerta used their voices to give voice to the voiceless. Dr. Martin Luther King, Jr. used his voice to help a nation dream. Gandhi freed a nation through *peaceful* revolution, never firing a shot, all through the *power* of his voice.

I'm not telling you that you can change the world as these individuals did; I'm only telling you that you have the opportunity to change your life right now, forever. In this book you will discover what power you have within you and how to access it.

You'll discover that how you think about yourself, what you consider your self worth can alter your life, how your work ethic matters, and that you should never let someone else put you in a corner where you *know* you don't belong.

Ask questions. Believe in the mark. Remember, what worked for me may not work for you. Your life is unique, it's beautiful, and it's *powerful*. So let's start challenging what you know. Let's start asking those important questions, let's see where life is about to take you, and let us never forget that our voices are our power.

Let them be heard!

"Knowledge is Power." — Francis Bacon

WHAT IS POWER?

What is power?

We often think of power as being good or evil. It's as though a person who has power is controlled by it, manipulated by it, and is at its whim.

Power is neutral, though. It is neither good nor bad. It simply *is*.

Let me offer you a single word and think about it for a moment ...***nuclear***.

When you think of nuclear power, what comes to mind? Is it the power of a nuclear bomb? That's reasonable and what most people tend to think about when they hear that word. Power. But what about a nuclear power plant? That's powerful, too.

Yet one is designed to destroy while the other is designed to build up. A nuclear power plant produces electricity that we use every day in our cities and towns. Without electricity, we wouldn't be able to use our computers, watch TV, listen to our iPods, talk to our friends on the phone, or many of the other things we take for granted. That's pretty good, isn't it?

Power is the *ability to get things done.*

Okay, so power is neutral. It doesn't live with the Dark Side of the Force nor does it serve the Good in the world. It simply exists.

Throughout history, men and women have left a trail of destruction in their path because they sought to dominate others. They were either handed power through a birthright, like a king or queen, or they obtained it by *influencing* others for the purpose of seizing control over them, like Hitler.

Push people around, threaten them, and be a bully and you'll get a few who like you, think you're pretty cool and tough, and others who are scared of you. But what do you have? You don't have any real power. You have fear. That doesn't influence anything or anybody. That just moves people out of your way.

When I talk about the power of youth, I'm not talking about a way to become strong so you can stand up to people who have hurt you. I'm not talking about lifting weights and being tough. I'm talking about making a difference.

Being a positive force in the world around you.

In order to change the world, in order to change the world around you, to inspire, to influence others, and to leave a true mark on the world, you need to have power. How you get it and what you do with it are generally intertwined and I want to share the tools necessary to take those steps to becoming powerful in this book.

When I talk about power, I want you to think about a positive force in life, something that will help you change your life, that will help you change other's lives. Forget about how big or small you are. Forget about how tall or short, skinny or fat, or what kind of grades you currently have in school. Forget about where you came from, what neighborhood you live in, or whether you have a broken home or not.

Power is available to everyone. It all starts with you.

It doesn't matter where you come from or what tools you're given; you can gain knowledge and power from anywhere. Jay-Z was asked one day whether he felt uncomfortable in a roomful of lawyers and doctors, men and women with advanced degrees and he said no, he did what he could with what he had access to at the time.

He wasn't rich, didn't come from a great neighborhood, but he *knew* that he needed more knowledge to climb his way out of where he was. So he used the one thing he had: his voice. With his voice, he gained knowledge, which eventually led to access to more knowledge and so on.

To have true power, you must have a lot of knowledge. *OR*, you must know that you have a lot to learn.

Power is the ability to get things done and in order to get things done you must have knowledge. Power is, at its most basic:

- *Who you are*
- *What you believe*
- *What you know*
- *What you are worth*
- *Who you know*
- *What you do*
- *What you say*
- *How you use it*

Are you thinking about yourself, your life, and what you want to do with it? Where do you see yourself in one year? Five? Ten? What do you want to be?

You may not have a clue right now about what you want to do in life, and that's fine. Knowing that you have a lot to learn is the first step to knowledge, and the first step to power. Knowing who you are is the next step.

Be mindful of facts. Don't be afraid to ask questions. And remember that the more knowledge you have, the more potential power you hold. What you do with all of that determines how powerful you become. So to sum it all up, power is about you. It all begins with you! So let's get started.

What Is Power?

QUESTIONS TO CONSIDER

- Why is it important to have power?

  _____

  _____

  _____

- How can power help you change the world?

  _____

  _____

  _____

- What are some ways you can be a powerful force in the world around you?

  _____

  _____

  _____

ACTIONS TO CONSIDER

Who's got the power? Create a list of five people who have used power in positive ways.

- What did they do? Why was it positive?
- What characteristics did they exhibit that you would like to have?
- Try to incorporate those characteristics in your life.

"Regardless of who you are or what you have been, you can be what you want & need to be." – W. Clement Stone

POWER IS WHO YOU ARE

Who are you?

It's a simple question, right? If I ask you that simple question, what's the first thing that pops into your mind? Let me guess ... your name, right? But that's not really *who you are*. Your name is a symbol, a designation, a representation of who you are. *It's not who you are.*

Your name is only a way for someone to identify you. 'Hey, there's Carlos.' Or, 'Carlos, hang on a sec.' You answer to your name and people who know you will immediately have some thought, some impression about *who you are* based on hearing that name. But your name really isn't who you are. So, let me ask you again: *Who are you?*

It's a tough question for many people to answer, but more so when you're younger because you're still trying to figure it all out: what you like, what you want to do, where you fit in. Heck, you're still discovering the immense possibilities that surround you in this life. How difficult it is to answer this question reveals just how important it is.

It's a foundation for power in your life. If you want to have power -*true* power and not the kind where people fear you, but rather where people *want* to listen to you, *want* to be around you, and *want* to help you- then you need to truly understand the power of **who you are**.

The power of who you are is all about:
- **The Look and Feel**
- **The Hustle**
- **The Straight Shot**

.

The Look and Feel

You never get a second chance to make a first impression, so let's start with the look and feel. Who would you like to ~~hook up~~ -I mean- hang out with? A big, burly 450-pound sumo wrestler or the Wicked Witch of the West (from *The Wizard of Oz*)? Or maybe someone who looks like Brad Pitt, Jessica Alba, Drake, Tyler Lautner, Selena Gomez, Gabrielle Union or some other polished celebrity? Who would you want to be around? Who would be your first choice? Sure, there are probably people out there that would pick the sumo wrestler or have a thing for green-faced wicked witches from the West, but most of you would pick those others. So here's my question to you: Why?

You don't know them. You don't know their personalities. You have only a limited perception of who they are, but your decision is likely driven by one factor: they're '*hot.*' In other words they are attractive.

There have been numerous studies through the years that have proven that attractive people enjoy more opportunities in life than less attractive people. This, of course, is in no way fair, but it is a reality we have to be aware of. Does that mean that if you are like me and would not consider yourself traditionally good looking, or maybe you're big-boned, that you can't control whether you're attractive or not? Absolutely not. You are in *full control* of whether you are attractive or not.

The Look is more than just the physical, it's more than genetics; it's about how you present yourself to the world.

Do you dress in a manner that conveys to people whom you wish to be? That doesn't mean you have to wear a suit and tie (though there is a time and place for that). But it does mean that you should care about how you dress and look. It's a representation of your style; a representation of your personality, a representation of who you are, an extension of you. If you want people to take you seriously and listen to you, having no regard for what you wear isn't going work.

Do you have good hygiene? How many of us know someone whose breath is so horrid it singes the hair off your eyebrows? Does that make you want to get closer to them or farther away? Or, like most people, do you keep your distance? Personal hygiene is just as important as how you dress. It's a representation of how much you care about yourself. If you have bad breath, do what I do and carry around gum to freshen your breath when you need it, which is about every hour or so for some of us. Everything I do in regard to hygiene is purposeful. The cologne I wear, how I shave, the gum I use, the gel I use in my hair, even the fact that I gel my hair is all for the purpose of bringing people closer. I make those choices; *you* make those choices. You make the choice whether to keep your hair neat, shave, brush your teeth, floss, dress the part, and so on.

If my hair was a mess, if I had body odor and looked dirty and if my breath smelled like hot garbage, that would *repel* people and that's *not* power.

And then there's personality. How you carry yourself is part of the *look* and attractiveness that you offer people. Are you excited? Are you fun to be around? Or are you that person who drags people down with you. 'It's raining again. Why does it always have to rain? I'm so sick of the rain. It never stops raining.' Blah, blah, blah.

Get out there and dance in it! "Yes! I love the rain. Listen to the music it plays as those raindrops splash in the puddles." Okay, maybe take an umbrella with you. But enjoy life. We only have one. And regardless of what you may be going through, no matter the circumstances, a life is always better than no life. And while you may not be able to dictate the circumstances, you are able to dictate how you engage those circumstances, how you engage your life. Be the change. Be the person that is friendly, that is uplifting, that is inspiring. Be fun, be exciting, and attractive. Be you, the best you can be.

Your appearance is only half the battle, though. How many of us know some incredibly, *physically* beautiful and attractive people out there who are mean, miserable, conceited, or just plain annoying. I don't care who you are ... if you're not enjoyable to be around for more than 5 minutes, if you make people feel bad, you have limited power.

How you make other people *feel* is just as important, if not more so than how you **look**. One of my mentors once told me that people may forget what I look like, they may forget what I said, they may forget my name, but they will never forget how I made them feel. Do you make people feel wanted? Safe? Like they matter? Do you listen when they talk to you or do your eyes and attention begin to wander? Do you remember their names? That's a big deal.

Remember at the beginning of this chapter when I asked you who you are and we assumed that the first thing that popped into your head was your name? It's important to you. Why wouldn't it be important to others as well?

If you can't remember someone's name five minutes after you just met them, how do you think that makes them feel?

When I go to a fast food joint, a restaurant, or anywhere else where the employees have nametags, I pay attention to them. I say their name. 'Thanks Sandy, have a wonderful day,' I might say while taking my order. Or 'Steve, you're doing a great job. Keep it up.'

I smile and am polite. I give people compliments whenever I can. I try to do nice things for people, random acts of kindness, for no other reason than to make them feel better. I treat people the way I want them to treat others, to treat my family, to treat me.

People *feel* good when they're noticed, respected, appreciated and they will tend to remember you, and they will in turn treat others the way you treated them. Pay it forward. That's power. But don't give false compliments just for the sake of trying to win favor. If you think their rainbow wig looks hideous, you don't have to say so, but don't tell them it looks awesome. Be kind, be compassionate, but always be real.

The way you ***look*** makes people want to come to you. The way you make them ***feel*** makes them want to stay. This is a part of personal power. The way you cultivate your look and develop the way you make people feel when they're around you will determine your level of personal power. Once you have that down, then you're ready for the **hustle**.

The Hustle

How much effort do you put forth in your life?

- 25%?
- 50%?
- 100%?
- 125%?

"Now, Carlos," I can hear you thinking, "no one can give more than 100%. It's not mathematically possible."

Yes, it is. You can go beyond 100%. It's all about **hustle**. Successful people will tell you that they got where they are in life because of their effort, their hustle. There is no such thing as an overnight success. Behind every so-called "overnight success" there are years of practice, sacrifice, education, training, dedication and preparation; in other words **hustle.**

After I left my corporate job to pursue my true passion of working with students and in the education field, I got my first job in the admissions office of a university. I had no business getting that job. I really wasn't qualified for it, nothing in my education or experience made me an ideal candidate on paper, heck I hadn't even volunteered to do admissions work while I was in college. But I really wanted the job. So I prepared for my interview. I researched the position online, found sample interview questions, called friends that worked in admissions at other schools to gain some better insight on the position, learned about the school, set up mock interviews with friends so I could be ready; I practiced, I trained, I prepared, I **hustled.**

I got the job. But getting the job wasn't enough. I had to excel. This wasn't just a job; this was my passion. I really wanted to do well, so I watched my boss. He came in around 7:45 in the morning every day and left around 4:30 in the afternoon. So I came in at 7:30am and left around 5:00pm. There were days I arrived earlier and stayed much later, but overall, that's what I was doing.

I discovered that I could get so much done in those 15 minutes in the morning and afternoon because there was no one else around. No emails coming in, no gossip about NBA Basketball Wives or whatever. It was during that extra time, that I began to do exactly what had gotten me the job in the first place: **hustle.** It was an unexpected by-product, but you know what? Every time my boss came in, he saw me already there. Every time he left for the day, I was still working.

I gave off the impression of being a go-getter. I was getting things done and if there was a big project coming up, guess who got it?

That's right. Me. Now, if I was the type of employee who always showed up late, left early, and had an excuse every time, who gave about 80 or 85% effort, would I have been successful? Odds are no.

How much effort do you put into your life? How much do you put into school, work, family, and friends? If you put in 85%, that's exactly all you'll get back. Have you ever wondered why you're only getting so much out of life yet? Look at the effort you're putting in.

There's an awesome movie out there called Gattaca. In this movie, people are genetically engineered to be superior. Yet one man who is not engineered wants to travel to space. The problem is that non-engineered people are only given the lowly jobs such as janitors and such.

He decides to assume the identity of a genetically engineered person, goes to extreme lengths to fit in, and strives to be as good -and even better- than those so-called 'perfect' specimens.

When he competes against his police officer brother in a swim race, he ultimately wins and the brother wants to know why. His response was something to the effect of, 'because every stroke you made, you were saving one stroke to get back to shore. I never saved anything for the swim back. I was putting it all out there." He hustled.

The effort you put forth determines what you get back. Hustle is all about effort and effort equals dependability. So if you've got the look and feel, meaning people are attracted to you, like and want to be around you, and now you show that you are dependable and will consistently hustle, especially when it counts, that's powerful. Not only will people like you, but they will depend on you.

Do you see where the pieces of **who you are** start to fall into place? The way you look, the way you present yourself and how you act, the way you make people feel, and how much effort you give to them and the things that are important in life all makes a difference in the end.

It all gives you *power*.

The Straight Shot

Now for the straight shot. You absolutely *must be a person of your word.* Integrity.

It builds trust and that is one of the most important foundations of any relationship in life. Without trust, without integrity, you have nothing. Be a person of your word.

If you can't do something, don't say you can. And don't say you 'can try.' In the immortal words of Yoda, the wise Jedi master, 'Do, or do not. There is no try.'

To *try* is to assume failure. To *do* is to accomplish.

If I disagree with something you're saying or doing, I'm going to tell you. But at the same time, you'll know I've got your back. Integrity.

John Edwards. Know who he is? To this day, he is still one of the most despised people in this country. It was just four years ago when he ran for president and was a front-runner in the Democratic primaries.

Then revelations came out that he had cheated on his wife. Not only that he cheated on her, but that he did so while she was battling cancer. Not enough for you? He got this other woman pregnant, said it was his campaign manager's affair, and then spent millions of dollars of his campaign funds trying to cover it up (see how I used the word 'try' there?).

No integrity whatsoever.

If you don't take your word seriously, you won't have the personal power you need to change your world.

If you do take your word seriously and always live up to it, then people will trust it, people will go to war for you, they will live for you, and they will die for you.

That's power.

Never over-promise something you know you can't deliver. Say what you will and be sure that you *can*.

Who you are is all incremental. If you are attractive –your **look**- (if you are neat, clean, presentable, etc.), people will come to you. If you make them **feel** good, they will stay with you. If you **hustle**, people will notice and turn to you more often for guidance and help, they will depend on you. And if you give them the **straight shot,** they will trust you and believe you and more importantly the will believe *in* you.

Who you are is so much more than your name. Who you are is up to you. What you do, the choices you make, the person you choose and strive to be. All of it is the sum total of who you are and makes your name more than a symbol, more than just a designation, it makes it powerful. Forget what you were, forget what you think you are, and look ahead to who you will become. **Powerful**.

Power Is Who You Are

QUESTIONS TO CONSIDER

- What does the phrase "you never get a chance to make a first impression" mean?

  _____

  _____

  _____

- How much effort do you put into the things that are important in your life (school, family, friends, etc.)?

  _____

  _____

  _____

- How can a lack of integrity hurt someone?

  _____

  _____

  _____

ACTIONS TO CONSIDER

Go out and do something nice for someone. Go to the New RAK City website (www.newrakcity.com) and learn about the power of random acts of kindness. Come up with an idea for a RAK. Download the New RAK City card. Do something nice for someone and then tweet @newrakcity how it made you feel to give a Random Act of Kindness.

"Purpose gives life meaning." – Charles H. Perkhurst

POWER IS WHY YOU ARE

The Purpose.

When I was a kid, I had no reason to go to college. I mean, absolutely none. People would ask me, "Carlos, what do you want to do with your life?" Or they would ask, "What are you going to study in college?" I had no clue.

Of course, you might be a few months from graduating high school or several years away at this point. You might not even *be* in high school yet, so the idea about having to answer that question wouldn't even come through your front door yet.

But it's an important one; no matter how old you are or how many years you have in front of you. So let me ask you right now that same question: *what do you want to do with your life?*

You don't have to answer it right now. Just hold onto it. Let me give you some common responses that I've heard through the years from people just like you and me and you can see if yours might be similar.

I want to help people.

I want to be a firefighter.

I want to be a movie star.

I want to make a lot of money.

I want to get out of this place.

These are all well and good, and there's nothing wrong with them. If you want to help people, that's wonderful. If you want to be a movie star, great. If you want to make a lot of money, that's fine, too. But there's something missing from these answers. One simple question: why?

Without the why, those answers don't provide *purpose* and purpose gives life meaning. You have to understand *why* you want to do those things or be those people.

If you don't understand your purpose, then you can't get out there and make it happen. You may want to be a firefighter. Okay, but *why*? Is it because your dad is a firefighter? Did you watch *Backdraft* and think how cool is must be to live that lifestyle? Is that enough for you? Why?

You want to get out of this place? Almost everyone feels at some time or another that they just want to get away from their hometown. They think that if they could just escape their neighborhood, then everything would be right in their world. But why?

And you know what the most common answer that we tend to give when pressed on the question of why is?

"I dunno."

And that's exactly what causes so many people to fail or quit. Not knowing your purpose, not understanding *why* you're out there doing something gives you an excuse to give up, to quit, to stop trying.

When I went to college, I had every reason to rationalize my failures early on. I had no purpose. I went through that first year, my freshman year, and proceeded to do as little as possible in class. I didn't care. For me, I didn't really know why I was there. I didn't have any purpose. I might have gone because it was expected of me.

But I didn't really care about it because I didn't know what I wanted to do with my life. So guess what? I wound up on 'academic probation.' That's a fancy way of telling me I was two steps away from being kicked out of school because my grades were so poor.

How did that happen? The same way most of us get into those situations. You hear about a party or two on a Friday or Saturday night and you go to them. A couple of weeks later you're partying on Sunday as well. After all, it's still the weekend, right? You've got your justification. Then you've got to get the week started properly, so you spend time avoiding homework on Monday and kicking back with friends.

You add Tuesday to your routine because, well, why not? Wednesday marks the middle of the week, halfway to Friday, so that's reason enough to celebrate, isn't it? At college, many students only have classes from Monday through Thursday so it's just like the weekend all over again. Before you know it (before *I* knew it, at least), you're partying seven days a week and classes just aren't all that important anymore.

I had no purpose. I was drifting through life and there I was on academic probation. Big deal, right? Well, that's when I became Godfather to my cousin's son. That was one of those moments that changed my life. We all have them. You will too.

I was suddenly responsible for this young person, this new life. If anything happened to my cousin and the baby's mother, it would be my responsibility to care for this child. That was a big deal to me.

I decided to buckle down and apply myself. I had to turn things around. I went back there busted my butt. Improved my grades. Got involved on campus. I impressed my professors, got an internship, a bank job, and I was wearing a suit! Imagine me wearing a suit. That's a sight to see, let me tell you.

But I did it. I had purpose. I didn't know what I would do with my life yet, but I knew *why* I was going to work hard. For that little boy, my Godson.

Then the worst tragedy imaginable happened. We lost my Godson. He passed away. I was shattered. Devastated.

I went back to school but I didn't care anymore. I drank and eventually got kicked out. I was in a downward spiral with no direction, and I certainly didn't think I had any purpose anymore.

That's when my cousin, my Godson's father, intervened. He saw what had happened to me. He saw how the loss of his child affected me, and he wasn't going to just sit around and watch me self-destruct.

He helped me realize that I never lost my purpose. I had only abandoned it. I had found my purpose when I met my Godson and I thought that purpose was to be there for *him*, but in reality my purpose was to help children.

I decided to apply myself once more. I got back my scholarships, got back into college, and I was 'all in.' I was putting it all out there, laying my cards on the table, and determined to win.

We all have purpose in our lives. The problem is that too often we don't want to know what it is. We expect that we're going to fail. Maybe you've had a friend or family member, or maybe even a teacher tell you that you won't amount to anything, that you'll never escape who you are.

Those can be pretty devastating ideas to a young person.

So we tend to hold onto those beliefs, hold them in the back of our mind because it's easier to give up, to give in, and to quit when you believe that you were never going to make it anyway.

But when you have *purpose*, when you know what that is and you know *why*, then there is *nothing* that can stop you.

Nothing.

Okay, okay, so there are going to be some things that get in your way, but they don't stop you; they only make you alter your course a little bit.

When you're traveling down the road and run into some construction, do you turn around and go home? No, you take a detour and get back on the main road as soon as you can.

In life you might run into a roadblock or two (in fact, you will if you pursue your dreams and your purpose), but that will only stop you if you allow it to, if you don't know or believe in your purpose fully. 100%.

And how do we do that? How do we fully understand our purpose?

We ask the question, *why*. All the time.

Never stop asking the question why.

Brian Griese was a quarterback at the University of Michigan. He was the son of an NFL star and he wanted to follow in his father's footsteps, as so many athletes seem to do. He was asked why he wanted to play football. His simple answer was because he wanted to make a lot of money.

At first thought, that may sound pretty shallow, especially for a man whose father likely made a lot of money already. After all, he couldn't have had a hard life by any stretch of the imagination, right?

But then he was asked that important question *why*. Why do you want to make a lot of money? It turned out that he wanted to start a foundation that helped grieving families deal with loss. Why? He lost his mother when he was 12 years old.

That's purpose. While your purpose might be different, no matter what it is, as long as you know *why* it matters to you, then it's important. You can achieve it.

You want to be a movie star? Good. Why? Is it for the money, the fame, and the recognition? Is it because you find movies inspiring?

You want to make a lot of money? Why? To live a better life, to be more comfortable, to help people, to take care of your family? Why?

Know your why, know your purpose. Know your purpose, know your life's meaning.

Now, the question of why almost always leads to the question of how? Once you know what your purpose, once you know your why, you are going to want to do everything in your power to make happen. Understanding and knowing your purpose mandates its completion. But how will you make this happen?

The Motivation, The Triggers, and The Circles.

The Motivation

Think of your purpose as a destination, the general direction that you need to go. Now, think of your motivation as the driving force behind getting to that destination, pushing in the direction you need to go.

If you don't understand your motivation, or if you don't really have all that much motivation, then when you begin to pursue what you want to do, your purpose, it becomes that much easier to pack it in and give up when things get tough.

There is power understanding the things that motivate you, that drive you toward to success.

Tom Brady is the all-pro, future Hall of Fame quarterback of the New England Patriots. He's at the top of his profession, considered by some as possibly one of the best of all time. But that's not how it all started. Years ago, during the NFL draft, he and his family were led to believe that Brady was going to be drafted, possibly during the second or third round of the draft. But as the draft rolled on they just kept calling out other quarterbacks' names. At the beginning of the sixth round, Brady still hadn't been picked. I imagine he was beginning to feel like one of the last two kids to picked for a kickball game. He was the 199th player picked in that draft.

To this day, he gets emotional when talks about that day. How he couldn't take it anymore by the sixth round and went for a walk. How his family was there for him and supported him through that moment. He even cried talking about it during a national interview on ESPN. That moment became his motivation. It became his driving force.

You don't think that anytime his team is trailing late in the game with two minutes left, he doesn't dial up that memory, those emotions, that motivation. That he doesn't think to himself, "They didn't believe in me. I'm going to prove them wrong." That motivation has led to five Super Bowl appearances, three Super Bowl titles, a supermodel wife, a beautiful family and near legendary status. Tom Brady has a purpose and he has his motivation.

When I was in 10th grade, one of my teachers told me I would never amount to anything because, as he told me, 'You're the greatest piece of garbage I've seen.' That could have devastated me. That could have crushed me. Instead, I turned it into motivation. I wanted to show him just how far garbage could go.

Growing up watching my mother and father work so hard and sacrifice so much for my sisters and me motivated me to do well in school so that I could someday repay all that they had given me.

Watching the way my wife, who came from humble beginnings like me, struggled, persevered, and overcame any and all obstacles to achieve her life-long dream of becoming a doctor, all while being the most amazing wife to me and mother to our children, motivates me to be a better man, a better father, and a better husband.

Traveling across the country and seeing the light in the eyes of some of the students I speak to, motivates me to continue. Seeing that same light dimmed in others, because the same circumstances and situations I went through, motivates me to never stop.

Being counted out, being the underdog, my parents, my family, children; these are just some of the things that motivate me. They are pieces of my motivation. They drive me toward my purpose.

Cultivate your motivation. Rally it. If your family is your motivation, stay close to them. If you distance yourself from them, if you don't talk to them, you lose a part of that motivation that is so important. Identify your motivations, negative or positive, whatever they may be and grow them. Harness that power and use it to drive you toward your purpose.

But when you have your purpose and understand your motivations for having that purpose, then you have to figure out how to trigger those motivations.

The Triggers

What gets your blood boiling? What is it that people can say to you or do that will grind on your nerves, get you into a fight, make you say or do things you shouldn't and would probably regret?

Those are your emotional triggers and if you don't control them, then you are truly powerless.

When I was a kid, if someone said something about your mother, it was pretty much over. You were about to have a fight. You had to defend your mom's honor. Even now, kids tell me now that they get into fights because he said this, and she said that. They tell me how they were disrespected. They give me all the reasons and excuses in the world, and I've heard them all a hundred times over. But the truth is that they weren't in control. They were *reactive*, a slave to whoever was in control of the emotional trigger, the person who said this and said that, the person who 'disrespected' them.

Allowing others to know and control your emotional triggers is to allow others to gain control over you, to have power over you. In these moments, you are powerless.

Now you're probably telling me you wanted to do what you did. So let's see, you wanted to get in trouble, wanted to get suspended, wanted to say those hurtful things to your friends or your family, wanted to make a foolish, knee-jerk, reactive, emotional decision that you may never be able to take back and will always regret?

I didn't think so. But these are your 'triggers,' so to speak. So why let other people control them? Why can't you control them? Why can't you use them to activate your motivation and achieve your purpose?

Emotional triggers don't need to be negative. They don't have to just be about the things that rub your nerves raw, get you into fights, or make you say and do regrettable things. They can be positive. They can be about what pumps you up. What gets you excited? What inspires you? What **motivates** you? When someone else is in control of those triggers, we tend to react in a negative way. We tend to get angry and focus our energy on them. But what if you took control? Took that energy and turned it toward your motivations, toward your purpose? Then you'd have a powerful motivational force.

When I need to get pumped up for a speech, I listen to music. When I'm feeling down, I play with my two boys. When I'm gearing up to do something I've never done before, something where I'm the underdog, I watch the movie Braveheart or Rocky IV (him climbing up that mountain, enough said).   When I feel like I'm in a rut, I create something, music, speeches, designs, whatever ... I just create. When I need to get inspired, I read poetry, or watch spoken word, or talk to my wife. When I need to do something, to do *anything*, I trigger my motivations. *I trigger my power.*

When you have your purpose and understand your motivations for having that purpose and how to trigger those motivations, then you need to surround yourself with the people who will give you the *best* opportunity to achieve your goals.

All the while assuring that you will be in control of your emotional responses, and no one else.

The Circles

We are all surrounded by people who define us. Who you hang out with, who you're friends with, who you don't get along with ... these are all people who define you.

These are the people in your circles of influence. There are both negative and positive people in our lives and you need to start figuring out who they are, and in which circles they fall: positive or negative.

The negative people are usually the ones in your blind spots. You feel connected to them. You feel as though you need them, or rely on them, so you tend to look the other way when they do something or say something you don't like or agree with.

That's fine, except that they will tend to get in the way of your purpose.

You don't want to surround yourself with individuals that don't respect and support you and your purpose. Individuals that will give you bad advice, who may not always have your best interest in heart, that are selfish or tend to activate negative emotional triggers in you. Individuals that bring you down, that hurt you, that don't truly love or care about you or your purpose. These types of individuals will rob you of your power. And they will define you.

Positive, successful people surround themselves with positive, successful people. You want individuals in your circle that that inspire you, that respect and support you and your purpose.

That want to see you make your purpose a reality and will do anything in their power to help you. You want individuals in your life that will challenge you to become better. For example, if you play sports, you don't want to keep playing people you know you can beat. You want to play the best. Sure, you'll lose. A lot. But you'll learn a great deal more *from* them than you will by playing the easy competition just to notch another victory.

You need to manage the people in your life and surround yourself with people who have the skills and knowledge that you need in order to succeed in life.

Me and my wife make a great team because when one of us gets down (and you will get down plenty in your life), the other is there to lift us up, to tell us that we can do it, that we're going to succeed.

That's a major lift in life, to have those kinds of people surrounding you. What good does it serve to have people telling you to give up? Maybe they gave up or don't have purpose in their life, so they want you to come back down to their level.

No, you need to manage the people in your life, to manage your circles. If you don't, then you'll end up in the wrong place at the wrong time in the wrong circle.

Don't get me wrong ... that doesn't mean you have to turn your back on any of your friends. Never forget where you come from. It simply means that you should understand where they are in your circle of influence and whether they contribute positively or negatively toward achieving your purpose. Being able to achieve your purpose allows you the opportunity to go back to your friends and help them find and achieve theirs.

There's nothing you can't do in life. Forget anyone who ever told you differently. Surround yourself with family and friends who care and support you, role models who inspire you, mentors who guide you; create a circle that gives you the best support to achieve your dreams.

You will create your own circle of power. When you do that, you will know what you want to do with your life and realize that you *can* do it. Once you understand your purpose, you need to understand your motivation. Once you understand your motivation, you need to understand what triggers that motivation. Once you understand what triggers those motivations, you want to surround yourself with individuals who will trigger those motivations that will drive you toward your purpose.

That is the *why* of it all.

Power Is Why You Are

QUESTIONS TO CONSIDER

- What's your purpose? Why?

  _____

  _____

  _____

- What/who motivates you and why?

  _____

  _____

  _____

- What are your positive emotional triggers? (Listening to a specific song, watching a specific movie, etc.)

  _____

  _____

  _____

ACTIONS TO CONSIDER

Create your circle. Go and discover positive mentors to help you make your purpose a reality. Find an adult mentor (a teacher, a family member, a leader in the community.) Find a peer mentor, someone your age that you admire and look up to. Lastly, find someone younger than you that you can mentor. Build yourself a positive circle of influence that leads to success.

"Faith is taking the first step even when you don't see the whole staircase." – Martin Luther King Jr.

POWER IS WHAT YOU BELIEVE

How often do you hear something and it influences what you believe? Most of us shape our beliefs based on what we're told, what we see, rather than what we know.

There's a great scene in a movie called *White Men Can't Jump.* Don't laugh, it was an actual movie starring Wesley Snipes and Woody Harrelson.

Wesley and Woody are street basketball players, hustlers, Sidney and Billy, who bet other people to play them and try to win.

They don't like each other at all, but they realize that together they are unstoppable. In it there's a scene where Sidney takes Billy to a neighborhood basketball court and bets him that he couldn't dunk the ball. They're constantly trying to prove some point to each other and Billy has something to prove. Billy sizes up the basket, dribbles the ball, and jumps. He misses the dunk by inches. He tries again, but still can't get it. The stakes are high. He tries a third time and the ball bounces high off the rim. He lost the bet.

For the longest time, Billy tries to figure out what happened, why he couldn't dunk the ball. The truth finally comes out a few days later when he learns that the baskets are actually several inches higher than regulation.

The point is that Billy *believed* that he could dunk. He might have known that he could, but even after the first miss, he still believed that the basket was a regulation height and that *he* had done something wrong to miss the shot.

It matters what you believe.

The Inventory

I've been working with students for over fifteen years now and they never cease to amaze me.

As much as I teach them, at times I learn just as much from them. This one time we were working with a group of about forty students doing a cool little exercise called, 'What's with the hoola hoops?' It's one of my favorite icebreakers.

We split the groups into teams. Two teams compete. They stand in a circle holding hands and the object is to try and move a Hula Hoop from one person to the next, while holding hands, and without ever breaking the circle.

The teams race and the first one to get the Hula Hoop all the way around their circle wins. During the practice run, team one wins. We decide to do the best 2 out of 3. During the first run, team one wins again. The score is Team One – 1, Team Two – 0. During the next run we change directions and team two wins. The score is now tied. The last run will be the tiebreaker, winner take all. On the last run, the teams get to decide when their team will go. The last run was so close, closer than I had ever seen. But in the last seconds, team two comes from behind and wins.

It isn't until the end of the exercise when they realize that team two's Hula Hoop was actually smaller than team one's Hula Hoop. All things were equal except for the fact that team one had the obvious advantage of having a larger Hula Hoop. Yet, team two won. What if we told them from the beginning that theirs was smaller than the other? What would have been their reaction? Would they have won? Probably not.

They would have given up before they really had a chance. Why? It's called a self-fulfilling prophecy. When you believe that something can't be done, you aren't going to give it the same amount of effort that you would if you believed it were possible.

What you believe has power.

If you believe that you are going to succeed at something, then you will. If you believe you can't, then you won't.

That's why you should always take *inventory* of your beliefs. Take stock of what you believe about yourself, about others, about everything. You want to have a full understanding of what you believe and where you stand on things that mean the most to you, issues of consequence and matters of importance. You want to know where your beliefs stand in comparison with your purpose.

What you believe will make a major difference in your life, so check your inventory. If you believe that every hoop you have to jump through is too small and you're just going to get stuck, will you even try? Or will you breeze through with ease because you believe you can.

The Pages

When I was kid I loved to read comic books, but one thing that drove me nuts was that what was portrayed on the covers wasn't always necessarily what happened within its pages.

The covers were always designed to be provocative; to grab your attention and make you buy the comics even if the pages within were lackluster. I've got to admit, I fell for it a number of times and bought horrible comics based on the cover. But you have to go beyond the cover of the book to know what's inside. You have to go to the pages. It's all about what's between the pages.

Right now, as of the writing of this book, the country is watching one of the most contentious and bitter presidential elections in years. Yet the public is being fed tiny fragments of truth about either candidate. We're only being given the book cover, in a manner of speaking. It's up to us to get to the pages.

To really know what each candidate is about and where they stand on the issues. To make the best possible decision.

Have you ever heard the expression, *never judge a book by its cover?*

It means that you should never judge a person by his or her appearance. Nor should you believe anything just because someone else told you to. Open the book, check out the pages, then make your judgments, choose your beliefs.

When I went to college, I met this Norwegian guy. He became one of my best friends; we were even roommates. But in the beginning, talk about a culture shock for me. I mean, I grew up in the Puerto Rican section of Newark, New Jersey and was surrounded by people who were just like me for most of my life.

And here I was sharing a room with a guy from another country, with his pale complexion, blue eyes, and long blond hair. I had a certain impression of the world. It's what I believed at that time. Knowing him, though, changed my perceptions. It expanded my world and what I believed about it. If I hadn't known him, and hadn't become great friends with him, then I would have held onto those beliefs, beliefs that I had believed real because I heard them through other people, through the TV, and through my community. Meeting this guy proved all of that stuff to be wrong and taught me you shouldn't simply accept what others tell you as fact. Find out for yourself. Do your homework. Read the pages and don't just scan the outside jacket of the book.

The Quiz

You may have been taught all of your life certain beliefs. But at some point, in order to truly form solid beliefs that will define you, you need to go beyond them. You need to question them.

Question your belief system. I don't care if it's about religion, politics, people, school, or even your best friend. Question it.

What do you believe? Why? What makes that belief hold up? If you believe in God, great. Why? Is it because that's what your parents believe? Is it because that's what you've been told all your life in church?

Some say questioning your faith and beliefs is wrong, but I don't subscribe to that. Now I'm not advocating turning your back on what's important to you, but only to question that which you don't fully understand. If it stands up to your questions, then it's strong. Question them now; prepare them for when you will need them most.

Your beliefs will become your center. It doesn't matter if someone else might consider them left or right, right or wrong, up or down, because it's *your* center. And when you approach life and pursue your goals and dreams, you need your center to be rock solid. Because if your center isn't strong enough, if it's based on beliefs that are thin, that haven't been tested, you'll question them at a time when you should be gathering strength from them, or worse, you'll find yourself giving up.

Question your beliefs. If they are strong, if they are true, then they'll pass the quiz and you'll be ready for the mountains ahead.

The Mountains

Everywhere you turn in life, you'll be facing mountains. Not physical mountains, but figurative ones.

They always come in pairs. There are always two. Fake ones and real ones. When I was in tenth grade, I began to seriously struggle in school. That was when I began to really lose my way. Getting in trouble, hanging with the wrong crowd and just basically screwing up. It didn't help that some of my teachers didn't see much potential in me. One of my teachers even called me the greatest piece of garbage he had ever seen in his life. I was told that I would never graduate high school, let alone ever go to college. I had certain friends telling me that all we were good for was getting into the trouble we were getting into. As a result, I began to believe them.

But here's the thing, from the moment you are born until the day you die, someone will always try to label you. Short, tall, fat, skinny, troubled, gifted, smart, dumb, athletic, clumsy, success, failure. They will always try to label you. It's up to you to decide whether or not you will live up to the labels that they are trying to put on you. Or whether you tear those labels off, rip those labels up and throw those labels away. You can never, ever let anyone tell you who you are or who you will become, because that is your destiny to fulfill. Never, ever let anyone define you. *You* define you. Period. End of statement. But nobody told me that, until the twelfth grade.

My senior year I met two crazy women: a crazy guidance counselor and a crazy admissions recruiter.

Between the two of them, they were convinced that I belonged in and was going to go to college. They were tireless. They chased me down, badgered me, continuously bombarding me about everything that had to do with college.

They even called my house and got my parents involved. They took me on a trip to visit a university. They made me take my SATs. They believed in me. Suddenly all the negative things that people had said about me became whispers. The labels I'd been given began to fall off. They were replaced by new labels: college bound, successful, powerful. Those ladies believed in me and when we received my SAT scores, their belief was validated. I had scored well enough to attend almost any school in my state. I scored enough to get some scholarships. It wasn't that I lacked potential, but my potential wasn't tapped. It wasn't that people didn't believe in me, it was that I didn't believe in myself. Those amazing women help me believe in myself.

I got accepted to every school I applied to. And I looked out to the horizon of my life and I saw two mountains before of me. Both equal in size, both equally intimidating.

There was no way I could overcome one mountain, but two was impossible. I began to doubt myself. The whispers were getting louder. Then on graduation night, after I had received my diploma, as I looked for my family in the crowded gym, I began to get emotional.

The crowd suddenly parted and I saw something I had never seen. My dad was crying. He hugged me, grabbed the back of my head and brought our foreheads together so our eyes would meet. He looked into my eyes and said, "You are my son. The son of Carlos Ojeda. You can be whatever you want to be, go wherever you want to go and do whatever you want to do, as long as you choose to." Then he said, "Go." And I went.

And as I, again, turned back to the two mountains before me, they were still intimidating. But it is in the moments when you feel you can go on, where you feel that obstacles before you are insurmountable, it is in those moments that you overestimate and underestimate your resolve. You are strong; you are powerful, if you believe.

It was then that I realized that one of the mountains was fake. It was made up of all the pain, doubt and fear I had in my heart. It was held together by all the people who didn't believe in me and all the things they had said about me. All the labels they tried to label me with. This mountain wasn't real; I had allowed its creation. I gave all that pain, doubt, and fear form. I gave all the non-believers and doubters power. I had created this mountain to prevent me from ever tackling the real one. So if I built it, if I created it, then I would be the one to tear it all down. I had to tear it all down so I could chase down the real mountain, which was to go to college and graduate, climb it, overcome and conquer it. Because conquering that mountain, gives you power.

The experience of overcoming your fear and obstacles makes you stronger. And once you are on top of that mountain, you'll be able to see that the world is much larger and that there are many more mountains out on the horizon waiting for you to conquer them. And conquer them you will, because once you conquer one, you can conquer them all.

In life you have to chase the mountains, tear down the fake ones and climb, overcome, and conquer the real ones. That's power.

So you might be in ninth grade and graduation looks like Mount Everest (if you don't know what Mount Everest is, find out. Knowledge is power). It might appear to be a mountain that is simply too high to climb, too vast to get around.

But you *can* climb it. Do this: get a pad of Sticky notes and begin to write down anything and everything that you don't believe you can do or that someone has told you is impossible. Place those on your wall. Line the first few up from left to right. As you think of more, place them above this line, but one less than the line below it, so that you begin to form a triangle-like shape. Eventually you'll begin to see a mountain forming in front of you.

So many challenges. So many things that you can't do. Take a step back and look at them all. Pick one and take it off the wall. No matter what it is, begin to write a list of reasons why you *might* be able to actually do it.

Then write down possible ways that you could do it. If you were told you'd never be a professional basketball player, write down 'practice, dedication, exercise, find a coach, mentor, tryout for the varsity team,' or anything else you can think of that would put you closer to achieving that goal. It doesn't mean you *want* to; it's just to get that Sticky note off the wall.

As you work through the notes, you'll begin to realize that almost anything is possible and that mountain is not really a mountain but a minor bump in the road, at best.

Anything is possible.

A child was born to a single mother who struggled to raise him in different places around the world and he overcame large odds to become the first Black President of the United States. Yes, anything is possible.

You need to chase down those mountains and tear down the ones that don't exist and overcome the ones that do. When you do, you'll begin to understand the power of belief.

When you believe in what's possible, the things that are impossible don't matter anymore. The stronger your beliefs, the more *powerful* you become.

Power Is What You Believe

QUESTIONS TO CONSIDER

- Why is it important to believe in yourself?

  _____

  _____

  _____

- How can certain beliefs keep you from gaining power or experiencing success?

  _____

  _____

  _____

ACTIONS TO CONSIDER

I believe in me. Paste your favorite photo of you in the middle of a sheet of paper. Underneath the picture, write I believe. Then fill the paper with positive adjectives or other words to describe you. Ask family and friends for their input.

Thank you for believing in me. Who believes in you? List all the people in your life that believe in you that support you. Then write them a thank you note. Thank them for their support and let them know you appreciate them.

"Knowledge will forever govern ignorance; and people must arm themselves with the power which knowledge gives." – James Madison

POWER IS WHAT YOU KNOW

Knowledge is power. The more you know, the more powerful you can become.

It's always been that way, yet for most of history, people in general have had limited access to knowledge. For thousands of years, there weren't even any books. People learned from others, or the church, or from their leaders.

Then books came along, but not everyone could read. Being able to read was a 'privilege' only the wealthiest could afford to learn. Then more children learned to read.

Now, though ... today, you have more access to information than any other generation in history of our world. Think about it, your generation, you, are more connected to knowledge than at any other time in history. You have more access to information at your fingertips than at any other time in history. Just open up your phone and you can find out anything you want about anything. But what do you do with it? You text each other:

-

The average teenager sends and receives 2,500 texts per month! Two thousand five hundred! Are you serious? That's 83 *per day*. But how many of them *gain knowledge* for you?

And there's nothing wrong with texting them. But let me give you a little insight into this thing called life. It's a game. This is all a game. We love games. That's why we play so many of them and root for our favorite pro teams. It's all a game and in life, the person with the *most knowledge* wins.

Knowledge is power.

It's the cornerstone of anything you will want to do with your life. When you listen to speeches about how to get things done, how to be great leaders, and how to achieve your dreams, you'll hear the same line over and over and over. Knowledge is power.

Without knowledge, you can't be prepared. You can't understand the steps that you need to take in order to go after what it is you want.

It doesn't matter if you don't know what you want right now. But someday you *will* know and when you do, you'll need knowledge to help you go after it.

There is power in what you know. So play the game. Play to win.

The Game

If you had to study for a major science test, who would you rather be? Any cast member from the Jersey Shore? Lindsay Lohan? Pee Wee Herman? Or would you rather be Albert Einstein?

I bet you chose Einstein. Why? Because, as they say, he was *smart.* But come on, we live in a time where it isn't 'cool' to be smart. We live in an age when ignorance, as they say, is bliss. The people on Jersey Shore aren't famous because of their IQs; moreover they are celebrated for being dumb and ignorant. We don't celebrate knowledge anymore.

We idolize the Kardashians, Snookie, and Lindsay Lohan for what they don't know. As if knowledge is not needed to be successful, to be powerful.

But that's not reality. Success is like a game. It's all a game and in life, the person with the *most knowledge* wins. So if you've got a science test, you know you are choosing Einstein. Because he was smart and knowledge is power.

Yet he didn't get to be smart by sitting around ignoring information that gives us knowledge. He pursued it. But what's more amazing to me is that even as all of these kids -maybe you included- agreed that they'd rather be Einstein because he's smart, nine out of ten don't choose that path. They don't pursue knowledge.

Did you know that Einstein wasn't a great student? Did you know that he had a speech problem? He didn't say his first words until he was almost three years old! Albert Einstein was an average student at best. He got by, but little else. He even *failed* his college entrance exam.

But he sought out knowledge. He was a patent clerk and working on his own free time on theories that would eventually change the world of science and the world in general forever.

He could only do those things by seeking knowledge. He read about other physicists and the theories they were working on. He studied mathematics and equations. He connected with researchers and professors to find out everything he could about his own theories and how to make them work.

His knowledge gave him power and it was that knowledge that brought him attention that eventually helped him prove his Theory of Relativity. In the game of life, in the game of success, he won. He pursued knowledge.

Knowledge used to require a serious amount of effort to chase down. I'm serious. Once upon a time, in a galaxy far, far away ... okay, so it's not far away ... gaining knowledge required serious effort.

I know all about how tough it can be to feel as though knowledge is out of your reach. I remember when I was younger, in high school (stop ... it wasn't all that long ago), and I had to write a major report on some topic or other and I didn't have a clue what it was about. I was like, 'What?' But I knew the only way to find out was to pursue the knowledge required to understand it. And that's what I did.

I hopped on the bus, rode for what felt like an hour (though it was probably only ten or fifteen minutes) to the library, strode up those stone steps, between the columns surrounding the front doors, and into a building that was silent. I tiptoed in, searching for the librarian, this ancient woman who scared me more than anything else, hoping she didn't spot me and demand that I return a book that was late, one that I couldn't find anymore, and made my way over to the card catalogue system.

You're lucky ... you never had to deal with the card catalogue. This was a series of small drawers containing *tens of thousands* of small, index-sized cards. On each was listed information about every book in the library. Each card was one book. You saw the title, a brief description of it (if you were lucky) and where to find it in the library.

I'd gather my list of books and spend the next thirty or forty minutes tracking them down. If someone had taken the book out, I was out of luck. Then I'd have to browse through the book to see if it had the information I needed. I'm telling you, gathering knowledge used to require some serious effort.

Today we're more connected than in any other time in history. You have access to information on your computer, phone, tablet ... and it's always there, within reach, twenty-four hours a day, seven days a week. But what knowledge do you generate with it?

It's all about the game.

We love competition. We love games. It's the easiest way for us to measure success against other people. We all want to be better than others. We want to win. In the game of life, the more you know, the more you *win*.

But the problem is that it's too easy to say, 'I don't know' to certain questions. Let me give you a simple example.

What's the capital of Zimbabwe?

I don't know, right? That's reasonable. But here's the catch: there's no excuse to not be able to find out in a matter of seconds. Take out your phone or open the Internet on your computer, type into a search engine 'Capital of Zimbabwe' and see what happens.

Bam. Pow! You've just *gained* knowledge.

Let's try this again:

- o What's the periodic table designation for lead?
- o What is the quadratic formula?
- o Who is the current treasury secretary of the United States?

Find out.

You see what happened? You found out and did so quickly. The words 'I don't know' should not exist in your vocabulary. Instead of 'I don't know,' say, 'I'm going to find out.'

Empower yourself with knowledge and the desire to find out.

Attainment of knowledge is one thing. It's only one half of the battle, the battle to win this game. Application of knowledge is the other half.

You could know a tremendous number of facts but if you don't know how to apply that knowledge, then it's not enough. Ask questions. Over and over, ask questions. What does that information or knowledge provide to you? How can you use it? Where does it benefit you or those around you?

When I first started out with this business, I didn't have a clue on where to start. So I went to the bookstore and got a book about the speaking business. I read it and immediately started applying some of the principles to my business.

I needed a promotional video, so I got a camera and went online and got some examples and began to film myself speaking. I needed some graphic designing and a website, but I didn't have the money to hire someone to design or build it for me.

So I download Adobe Photoshop, went to the bookstore, read about how to be a graphic designer and design websites, and then *applied* that knowledge I had gained into doing it.

That was one the secrets to my success. Acquiring knowledge and then applying it to my purpose.

When you apply the knowledge you've learned, you find more doors open for you in life.

You should never say I don't know; it should always be I'm going to find out. It should never be I can't, it should always be I'm going to figure it out. That's how I won the game. That's how you will win the game.

The Sources

So how do you acquire knowledge? We use the resources available to us. We use our sources. Our knowledge is only as good as the sources we use to acquire it. In order to expand our knowledge, we must expand our sources.

Read the newspaper, journal articles. Pick up a few magazines (or go to your library to read them for free). Subscribe to a blog. Wikipedia is great for pop culture, but it's not reliable for everything else, so be careful. All sources are not created equal.

The source of your information is important. If you're talking politics but your only source of information is MSNBC, you're getting a slanted, biased viewpoint, not a balanced, factual assessment. The same holds true if you only watch Fox News.

Find sources that help you gain knowledge. If I ask you where you get your information right now, you might say Facebook, family, friends, and teachers. There are so many more, such as the library, Twitter, books, family, TV, news, online resources, and much more.

The *more* sources you have, the better your knowledge base becomes, and then you'll be able to make better decisions.

A friend of mine once gave me a movie recommendation. I downloaded the movie and watched it as I was flying home from a speaking engagement. It was the worst movie I had ever seen. So bad, I contemplated jumping out of the plane to make it stop. That person was put on my 'never watch a movie recommended by this person, EVER' list. They were not a good source for movie recommendations. Now I use Rotten Tomatoes.com and a circle of friends whose opinion and recommendations I trust.

It doesn't matter the decision, whether it's trivial or critically important you want to have solid sources. Whether it's what movie to watch, what to wear, or important decisions like where to go to college or what career to choose, you want good, varied, credible sources of information.

With narrow sources of information, you make narrow-minded decisions. If you want to be successful in life, choose broad sources of information. There are so many sources of information to choose from, just waiting for you to tap into them. If you want to be a person of conviction, and you want those convictions to stand the test of time, you need to make sure they're based on broad, reliable sources that are tried and true and tested again and again.

Knowledge is power, but you're only as powerful as the broadness and the vast expansiveness of your knowledge.

The Facts

Ever hear someone say, 'I'd be right if it weren't for those pesky little facts'? Facts are absolute truths. They can't be altered, denied, or twisted around.

So many people, kids and adults alike, don't want to know the facts. They prefer to make decisions in a vacuum. Facts can make decisions more difficult.

You want to know some facts? If you knew some of the facts about high school dropout rates, you'd never consider dropping out. If you knew that you'd make $10,000 a year *less* than someone who graduates, would you dropout? If you knew that a dropout earns about $1 million *less* in a lifetime than a college graduate, would you dropout? Dropping out might appear like the easier option for some at certain times, but the facts highlight a tougher road in the long run. But when a person wants to do something, the facts get in the way, so they'd rather avoid them.

You have to embrace the facts, not to discourage you, but to give you the foundation upon which to be able to achieve your dreams. To plan on how to make them a reality. So many kids want to grow up to be professional athletes, basketball players. They think that dribbling a ball and shooting baskets for a few hours a week will get them in a position to have a shot.

But the reality is that *three* (3) out of every 10,000 high school basketball players will ultimately be drafted in the NBA.

But Chu, you're just trying to crush my dreams!

No I'm not! I told you to chase the mountains. I told you to tear down the fake ones, then climb and overcome the real ones. But if you don't know how big the mountain is, then how can you ever possibly plan to overcome it?

Look up Mount Everest (I mentioned it previously). How high is it? What does it take to climb to the top of that mountain? And how many people have died trying? Look it up. You'll find that information as well.

The air at the top of Mount Everest is so thin, climbers have to rest at a 'base camp' for up to three weeks so that their blood cells acclimate and can carry more oxygen to the body, because there's less oxygen available up there. If you simply marched on up there because *that's* what you wanted to do with your life, guess what? You'll fail. You might even get yourself into a dangerous situation.

You have to know as much about the mountain you're facing so that you can have the best opportunity to overcome it.

You've got to know the odds to beat the odds. You can't avoid the facts because it's easier or convenient. It won't change the reality that the real reason most people avoid the facts is because they're scared.

But fear is never a representation of the obstacle before you, but a representation of your perception of that obstacle. So it's fear and not the facts, not the odds that keep us from overcoming the obstacles in our lives. The only way to defeat fear and ignorance is through knowledge.

When you acquire knowledge and understand how to apply it, when you have vast, broad sources of information, you'll get the facts. When you have the facts, you understand what it will take to achieve your dreams. You plan, you chase down mountains, you climb them, you overcome them, and you succeed. You win the game.

Fear and ignorance lead to stupid decisions. Knowledge sets you free.

Power Is What You Know

QUESTIONS TO CONSIDER

- If you do not know something, how do you typically respond?

  _____

  _____

- Why is it important to know the facts? How can they motivate you?

  _____

  _____

ACTIONS TO CONSIDER

Check the source. Create a list of all your current sources of information. Now, brainstorm some new ones. Pick two and add them to your daily routine. For example, read the newspaper in the morning, or watch a video from TED.com everyday. Once it's a part of the routine, repeat this exercise and watch your sources of information expand.

Just the facts. Pick a topic (science, history, math, etc.) Make sure the topic is something your interested in. Challenge yourself to learn one new fact about the topic every day for thirty (30) days. Knowledge is power.

"Self-worth comes from one thing - thinking that you are worthy." – Wayne Dyer

POWER IS WHAT YOU ARE WORTH

There is power in what you're worth. So ... what are you worth?

Take a moment to think about it. If you're like most people, there's a word that first pops into your head when you hear that question. What are you worth? Okay, have you taken the time? Let me guess ... *money*.

Money is the one thing that people most commonly think about when they talk about their worth, or what someone else is worth. But you know what? Money is secondary.

I'll give you a moment to stop laughing. Take your time. Ready? Good.

Money is secondary. It's important, don't get me wrong, but when it comes to your worth, it's your *value*, your self-worth that is most important. What do you believe? What's important to you? What are your morals? Your ethics? Your skills? Those are all part of your value.

If you want to understand the importance of self worth, all you need to do is look to so many of today's celebrities. Lindsey Lohan is one of the best examples of a person who has no value in herself, has millions of dollars (money), but has no self worth. This is a young woman who is attractive, talented, and could have done anything she wanted to do in life, but she is also spiritually, emotionally, and on a power level, broke.

She's broke? Yeah, wouldn't we all like to be as 'broke' as her?

But I'm not talking about money. Like I said, that's secondary. Where do you think she's going to be in ten years? She can't get a job right now, can't get insurance, and few people in the business want anything to do with her. She is *powerless*.

Eventually the money's going to run out. All because her self worth is so low. When that goes, your power goes with it.

The Rich

Many of us dream of winning the lottery. We think that it will change our lives, give us the path to happiness, and that all of our problems will be solved. But you know what? That doesn't happen. Because people place more value on money than themselves.

Let's say I'm standing with a guy named Bob. We're both 25. Neither of us has much money. We're getting by, but barely. Bob works as much as he needs to, but keeps focusing on getting money the easy way. I believe in hard work, dedication, and my father's work ethic.

I have a talent I've discovered and am working to make the most of it. Neither one of us would be considered 'rich' by most standards.

He wins $1 million in the lottery one day. Great for him, right? He's rich and he's all set for life, right? Here's the thing, though: more than 7 out of 10 lottery winners go broke within 5 years.

Now let's fast-forward 10 years. We're 35. Bob is broke, struggling to earn some money and cover his bills. Money still consumes him. I've got a multi-million dollar business, a great family, and success.

I might not have had money when I was 25, but I had all the intangibles that lead to success.

I grew up poor in the sense of money, but I was rich in the sense of values, family, love, and grounding that made me who I am today. I was rich. You are rich.

I'll admit that it's tough today. We're a society that focuses on material things. You see $160 Nike sneakers and just have to have them. Why? Because it's supposed to be a reflection of your worth?

According to whom? Sure, we see Jay-Z and Kanye wearing certain things and just have to get the same clothing or jewelry or shoes. Why?

If you're always *needing* something, then you will always be powerless.

My grandmother, when she first immigrated to this country, didn't know any real English other than what someone had taught her to say when she walked into a restaurant, 'Ham, egg, and cheese.' That's all she ordered. As she got older, she'd slap you if you said that because she was sick of eating ham, egg, and cheese sandwiches.

But this woman went up and down the East Coast looking for work. She worked 13, 14 hours a day in the fields. She was like a modern day slave. She was getting paid a *fraction* of her real worth, but she sacrificed so that her kids would have the opportunity at a better life. That gave my father the opportunity to work hard, which taught me the value of hard work, family, and values.

Being rich is about having the intangibles in life that will help you achieve success. It's about creativity, skills, heritage, grounding, discipline, and all of that.

Money doesn't make you rich, but being rich will make you money. It's time for you to shift your definition of 'rich.' You need to begin to value yourself. Anyone can make money. But only truly rich people can make a life.

That's power.

The Conceit

Arrogance is destructive. Being humble is a very powerful tool. Just look at Chad Johnson (aka Ochocinco) or Terrell Owens of the NFL. These guys are notorious for their arrogance. As they reached their thirties, their speed and skills began to decline, as is natural, and they found it harder and harder to find a team willing to work with them. They were so arrogant for so long, it became a destructive force. Now, even though they want to keep playing, not a single team wants them. What power is there in that?

On the flipside, being humble to a fault, though, is not good either. Now, being grounded, down to earth and being able to laugh at yourself is cool. But when that starts to affect your confidence, your self-image and your self-worth, it begins to destroy your power.

Too many students have a habit of being humble and self-deprecating to a fault. You might look in the mirror and not see much to feel good about. You see the reflection of every negative thing anyone's ever said about you and you believe it.

But you have to believe in your worth. You have to believe and know that you're important. That you're valuable. I learned that the day my son was born. My wife and I were so excited. Our first child. Both our families were at the hospital waiting for any news. But after many hours of labor, there was a complication and the doctor decided that she would have to go in and surgically get the baby. Our excitement turned to nervousness. I was in the room, holding my wife's hand, reassuring her that everything was going to be okay.

Then suddenly, I heard a baby's cry and there was my son. When they placed him in my arms it was a moment of clear perspective and understanding. As I held him close, instant love at first sight, ready to protect and care for him, to die for him if I had to, I remember thinking, wow, my parents must love me this much." It was in that moment that I realized just how much my parents loved me, cared for me, how much they would be willing to sacrifice for me. I realized my value. You are valuable.

I look back on my life and am amazed that I'm still alive today. I didn't put much value in myself and ended up placing myself in dangerous situations, even well into college. I would be out at all hours of the night in dangerous neighborhoods. I came close to losing everything more times than I care to admit. But through my Godson's death, I learned to value life, and value my own life. And with the birth of my own child I realized my true worth in the eyes of those that love me.

I want you to take a moment and do something for me. I want you to have your parents and anyone else in your life that is important to you write a letter to you telling you what you mean to them. I want you to write one back to each of them as well.

When you read those letters, you'll get a different perspective on your value. You'll see yourself through someone else's eyes and that can be life changing. You might say, "Wow, I didn't realize" or "I had no idea you felt that way."

We often take our mother's or father's love for granted. We go through life (especially during adolescence) feeling as though our parents don't love us from time to time, or that they don't care and are just being mean.

It's the same wherever you go, but it's wrong. Like you won't know your mother's love (or your father's) until you have your own children. To be there when they're born, to hold them in your hands for the first time, it's overwhelming. You instantly understand the depth of your parent's love for you.

You need to value yourself, to believe in yourself, and find the balance between being humble and being confident. Never be cocky; being cocky is thinking you know where you are at, being confident is knowing where you've been and where you're going.

The Savings

Money will make you a slave. You have to get your money right. If you don't have any money and if you don't have any way to make money, then the only thing you'll care about is money. Instead of looking to the future with the hope of building a career, building a life or fulfilling a purpose, you'll be looking for a J.O.B.

A 'job' locks you down. It traps you. You dread going to work, punching in, and grinding through each day. It sucks. A career, a life, a purpose sets you free. A career, a life, a purpose is about pursuing your passion. But when you don't have your money straight, you won't be focused on a career, a life, a purpose but rather the job.

When you're preoccupied with money, life will pass you by. People want to save money. It's kind of the 'Duh' statement of the day, right? Who wouldn't want to be able to save? You want to have a bit of savings for that emergency or opportunity that might come along. That's a given, but money isn't everything and as I said earlier, having money isn't connected to your value.

Your experience in life should be the savings you value more. When you reach the end of your journey through this life, before you pass on to whatever you believe happens when we die, how much you have in your bank account isn't going to amount to a hill of beans. It won't matter.

What's going to matter are the experiences you have in your life account.

When I volunteered to speak and serve food at a homeless shelter for teens, my son asked if he could come with me. He wanted to help serve food. Teaching my son the value of service, working together to serve food and seeing the smile on this face, the joy he felt for doing something good for someone else, that was an experience in my life account.

When I took my two-year-old swimming for the first time, when I had to get in the pool with him and saw the smile on his face, that was an experience for my life account.

When my father hugged me when I graduated, that was an experience for my life account.

When my wife looked at me when I proposed and said, "I've been waiting for this moment since I first met you," that was an experience for my life account. Those are memories I will take with me wherever I go.

Those moments give you power. They give you value. The 'what you know' and 'why you are' and all of that … they all come from your moments, your memories. Those are the moments that you need to be saving.

Learn to value yourself and develop your own sense of self worth. Place the proper value on money and make sure that you understand there's more to life than money or material things.

You're worth a heck of a lot more than a piece of paper with the picture of a dead president on it. You are valuable. You are powerful.

7 Power Is What You Are Worth

QUESTIONS TO CONSIDER

- Why doesn't the amount of money a person is worth define his/her value?

  _____

  _____

- How do you define being rich?

  _____

  _____

- What are some experiences you can add to your life account?

  _____

  _____

ACTIONS TO CONSIDER

Shopping spree. You have $1,000 to invest in different aspects of life, such as money, power, success, family, education, religion and material possessions. How much of that $1,000 will you give to each aspect? Once you've place a value on each aspect, compare it to the amount of time you invest in the aspect in real life. Is it aligned? Is it off-balanced? What can you do to achieve balance between what you say you value and what you actually value?

"Success is all about people. It's about networking and being nice to people." – Mike Davidson

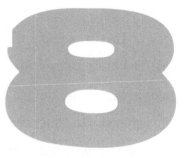

POWER IS WHO YOU KNOW

You are not an island. Even though we sometimes wished we lived on one, the truth is that we do not exist in this world in a vacuum, alone. We are surrounded by millions of other people and with social media we are closer to each other than ever before.

In 1967, Psychologist Stanley Milgram popularized the six degrees of separation theory with a study that asked 296 volunteers from Boston and Nebraska to get a document to a stockbroker in Massachusetts using only people they knew. Sixty-four letters ultimately reached their target in about six steps. But now, based on a study by Facebook and the University of Milan, the degrees of separation between two strangers is 4.74. So, basically if we were to randomly pick another person in the world, on average, you would know someone, who knew someone, who knew someone, who knew someone, who would know them.

This is a good thing. Because no one gets anywhere, no one becomes successful alone. We all stand on the shoulders of people that came before us that sacrificed so that we could have the chance to succeed. No successful individual has ever achieved it without the love and support of loved ones, the education and training of a teacher, the guidance and advice of mentors, even the random kindness of a stranger here and there.

Basically, your success, your power is the sum total of your power and the power of everyone you know, everyone that helped you. So if you want to be successful, you want to know people, who know people, who know people, who know people, who know what? People.

The Network

Who you know matters. Sure, you can have all the hustle, style, charisma, purpose, and raw determination that could fill a bus, and what you *don't* know will hurt you, but *who you know* – or better yet, *who knows you-* is very important.

What good will it serve you or anybody else if you're sitting there all alone? All that knowledge, all that power you've built ends up sitting there doing nothing when you're alone.

Networking is power. Just about everyone in this world knows at least someone else. So think about one friend you have. It could be your best friend, a casual acquaintance ... anybody. Do they know someone besides you? I bet they do. If you don't know that person, why not?

Maybe you don't like them. That's fine, but keep in mind that the more people you know (the larger your network), the more power you end up having.

When it comes to having power, everything is connected. Who you are, what you know, what you believe ... all of those things make a difference. Each of those, by themselves, makes you more powerful. But if you don't connect with other people, if you don't begin to develop *networks*, then there is nothing you can do with all that power.

It's about building your network. It's about who you know as well as who knows you. And I bet you're sitting there, just like me, and thinking about how much you can't stand the idea of networking. Getting out there, meeting new people, shaking hands, talking to strangers … it's a pain. Trust me, I know.

We're human beings. We prefer to stay within our comfort zone. It's a self defense mechanism because the unknown can be unnerving, or downright frightening. We are social creatures.

We want to be accepted, so we tend to have these thoughts in the back of our minds all the time, these little voices saying, 'What if they don't like me?' or 'What is they're smarter than me?'

We look at other people; especially those that have more experience in a certain aspect of life, and become intimidated. But you know what? Every single one of them started out in the same exact place that you're at now. Everyone.

But it's hard to see that at the time. We rely on that most basic defense mechanism and stick with the people we know. That's doesn't grow or cultivate your power.

There's a common phrase that Albert Einstein coined that goes something like this: *Insanity is doing the same thing over and over and over the same way and expecting a different result.*

As you grow, as you develop your power, as you increase what you know, find your purpose, strengthen your self-worth, solidify what you believe, then you become more powerful, but solutions to the problems you *will* face may come from other groups, other networks.

Networking is about taking that power you've developed so far and expanding it outward.

Social media –sites such as Facebook and Twitter- have been incredible tools for networking, but even Facebook, which is the largest single user site in the world, with almost 1 *billion* registered users, didn't begin with a sprint. It stumbled along at first and struggled to gain traction. Why? Because it *limited* a person's networking ability.

Facebook started out in Harvard by a student there, Mark Zuckerberg who kept the site for Harvard students only. Once they started branching out, they included a few other Ivy League schools, such as Yale and Dartmouth. But those users were limited to their own schools. This limited the networks that people could develop.

It essentially followed basic human nature, which is to stick with what you know. Yale students would stick with Yale students, Harvard with Harvard, and so on.

But once Facebook broke free of that bind, the site exploded in popularity. Now anyone can log on and connect with hundreds of millions of people from around the world. Talk about powerful.

But you can't just do it on Facebook. That's simple, but isolated. You're still little more than a stranger to people whom you meet on those sites. You still need to get out there and network face to face.

It's important that people know you. You could have five thousands so-called 'friends' on Facebook, but how many of them do you actually know? How many, if asked, could tell something about you? How many, if asked, could help you fulfill your purpose? Share their power with you?

Let me be clear, when you network, you're not looking for what those people *might* be able to do *for* you in the future, but to simply connect with them. Someday you might be able to do a favor for them, and that may or may not come back to you again, but if you *don't* know them, then the simple answer is that you won't be able to rely on anyone for anything and that is *not* powerful at all.

Let me tell you a story that took place years ago. I was married, working nine to five, my wife was in medical school, and we were broke. But to me, my anniversary was important. I wanted to do something nice for my wife on our anniversary. I wanted to go Big Time with it. But, like I said, I had limited funds.

Through networking years earlier, I knew someone who knew someone who knew someone who could hook me up at a nice French hotel at a price I could afford. So we drove into the city and pulled up in front of the hotel and the valet knew my name. My wife looked at me with this pleasant, but surprised look on her face, and I said, "That's what I do for the woman I love."

She simply said, "Shut up," in this perfectly playful way she has about her.

We went upstairs and the room was unbelievable. This thing was larger than our entire first apartment. We started going around the room, taking pictures, admiring the chocolate covered strawberries and champagne and let me tell you, it was like nothing we'd seen before.

Several years later we found those pictures and realized how 'ghetto' we were for taking them. We even had a picture of the bathroom!

But that wasn't all I had planned for that anniversary. There was a restaurant down the street with a long waiting list. No way I would get in. Not me, not some kid from the streets. But I knew someone who knew someone who knew someone who helped the owners get started. They got me a reservation at 5:45, before it opened for dinner service. I had to guarantee them we'd be out by the time they opened their doors, and I did.

I walked in there with my wife and it felt like the entire second floor of this place was reserved just for us. A music trio was rehearsing, came over and played for us, and I told my wife when she had that surprised and impressed look on her face, "This is what I do for the woman I love."

She simply said, "Shut up," in that perfectly playful way she has about her.

Then, I also heard that the Broadway show, The Lion King was in town. They were tough tickets to find. But I knew someone who knew someone who knew someone who had connections through public relations for the show. I got hooked up with some great tickets. Orchestra seats. We got to meet some of the cast members, got a playbill signed by the entire cast, and when my wife looked at me with that impressed, pleased look on her face, I said, "That's what I do for the woman I love."

And guess what she said in that perfectly playful way she has about her? That's right.

I wasn't rich. I barely had two pennies to rub together, but I had connections. None of them were direct connections, but they got things done.

I had *power*.

For the most part, people aren't going to make calls on your behalf and try to help you get something you need or want just because you're Facebook 'friends' or you follow them on Twitter. I know Justin Bieber but he doesn't know me.

I'm not being harsh. It's simply the hard truth that we need to accept. We need other people to get us to where we want to be. Without networks of people, all the knowledge and all the beliefs that we have won't mean much of anything.

Now, *how* do we build our network? We start by developing our elevator pitch.

The Elevator Pitch

The elevator pitch is a short statement that tells someone who you are. It's condensed down to the length of time it would take you to go from one floor to the next in an elevator.

Everything in your life should have an elevator pitch. Your life, your goals, your dreams ... everything. It should be this simple and concise:

Who you are, where you're from, what you do or what you want to do *and* why you are the bomb.

That's it.

Hi, I'm Jose. Currently I'm a bricklayer but I go to high school. I want to go to college so that I can learn to run my own business. Can you give me any advice to help me get started?

Bam! Done. Concise, to the point, and impactful. You'd remember Jose.

What if you walked up to a new teacher and said, 'Hi, I'm so-and-so, I'm a senior and I want to earn a certain GPA. What do I have to do to make that happen?' The relationship suddenly changes. Your teacher knows your name, what you want, and you have someone to turn to if you need help. Additionally, they are much more willing to give you the benefit of the doubt now that they know you. You've expanded your network.

If you don't represent yourself then who will? You might not need people in your network today or tomorrow or next year. You might never need them. But they're there when you do.

Now, let's work on that handshake.

The Shake

There are so many different handshakes out there I can't even keep up with them all anymore. There's the pound, the fist pump, and so on. Kids get so inventive that you need a special deciphering kit just to figure some of them out. They're ingenious. The problem is that 60-65% of people don't know how to shake hands properly.

You only get one chance to make a first impression and the handshake is a part of that impression. You don't want to give someone a reason to make a superficial assessment about you.

Some people, when faced with a handshake, don't know what to do. They end up shaking fingers. Well, you know what happens when you pull someone's finger? Imagine if you pulled all five!

The handshake is simple. Make the webbing between your thumb and index fingers connect with theirs. Dock. Embrace the hand firmly. Lock. You want to shake firmly, but don't crush their hand. Girls shouldn't do the curtsy handshake unless they're meeting royalty. And you shouldn't extend it too long.

Place your index finger by their wrist and when you feel that wrist move, let go. Make sure you give good eye contact. Don't stare, but look into their eyes. Deliver your elevator pitch, make sure to speak with you "outside" voice, let it project your confidence.

Dock, lock, shake, and let go. Simple, firm, done.

The Take

What do you take away from a meeting with someone? Don't say you'll remember them because you won't. You will for a few days, maybe even weeks, but when you meet a lot of people, you tend to forget others.

Ask for a business card. If they don't have one, make sure you have a piece of paper and a pen handy to gather their information.

Also, take the time to jot down any important information you learned about them on their business card once you walk away from them. Do they have kids your age? How about a sport they enjoy that you also like? Little things make a big difference. It's how we connect to others.

You also want to give your business card to them as well. Yes, you should have business cards with your basic information on them. Put your name and email on it. If you're a senior, it might be okay to put your phone number on it. If you do, make sure your voicemail message is professional. Also, while I don't want to limit anyone's style or form of expression, you want an email address that is simple, easy to remember, and has your name. Bigbadbootiedaddy@whatever.com may be cool to your friends, but it won't help you build your network. You don't have to turn that one off, but make sure you have one for your networks.

You can print your own business cards through stores like Staples or get free ones from VistaPrint.com and other sites. If you have social media pages, make sure they're clean. People have lost jobs, scholarships, and even families because they put the wrong stuff on their pages. If you have to create another profile, do it.

But make sure that you get as much information about the people you meet as you can. Make the 'take' work for you. Then follow up.

The Follow Up

It's one thing to get the cards and information from your networks, but it's another thing to not do anything about it. Follow up with each person you meet. Do it within 48 hours.

Write a simple email follow up, something general, and if you got any good information you can add, such as asking about their son who's in the same grade as you, do it. Anytime that you can make the general message more personal, you'll leave a better impression.

You might not get a response, but that's okay. They know you now. They'll remember you. If you want to stay in touch with them, do so by email every few months.

It can be tough to understand the power of networking at times. The larger your network, the more powerful you become. It took me a while to fully understand and appreciate that fact and I'd like to share a rather personal story with you. Hopefully you'll understand as well about the power of your networks.

My father was a dedicated and hard working man. I got my work ethic from him. One day he was hurt on the job. His employer refused to label it as a workplace injury, so Workman's Compensation insurance didn't cover his medical bills or time off. The employer actually took his vacation and sick time away for the days he missed when he went in for surgery.

My father sued them. He wasn't after money or a big, fat payday. He simply wanted his vacation time and sick days back, things he had earned through hard work.

The company refused and all the while my father continued to go to work and give his full effort on the job. My father won his case, was awarded Workman's Comp and the company was ordered to return his vacation time and sick days. They refused.

One day my father had a heart attack while at work. He was sent home. Not the hospital, but home. My mother ended up taking him to the hospital where he had a stint put in his heart to open his valves.

Now, I need to tell you that my parents are humble and proud people, they kept their problems to themselves. I'll probably get in trouble for even sharing this story. Like most parents, and probably like your parents, they wouldn't let their children know about anything they were struggling with. It didn't matter that we were adults; we were still their children. One day, several months after my father's heart attack, I went to their house aiming to steal a few cookies and some milk as I tended to do, but I found my mother crying instead. I asked her what was wrong and after a lot of coaxing, she finally told me everything.

They were struggling financially. They had missed too many paychecks while my father was recovering. This was a shock to me. My father even went back to work early to make money.

I was upset. I was confused. And I was angry. I went to my father's employer and all I got was a rude person telling me to get out of his office. All he saw when he looked at me was the son of a maintenance worker. I was nothing to him.

But I had a network. I knew people.

While every instinct in my body screamed for me to march back into that office and tear that guy a new one, I grabbed my phone, which had at least 15,000 contacts in it, from media anchors to senators and more, and started calling everyone I could. Newspapers, TV stations, councilmen, civil rights organizations, the Secretary of the State of Pennsylvania ... I rained on this guy's world. I brought hell down upon him.

Months later, the company finally gave my father all of his vacation and sick time back.

After my father had his second heart attack at work, those same individuals who answered my calls to help him out came to his funeral. It was about respect. And all of that happened because I knew people who knew people who knew other people and so on.

That's when I realized I had power.

When you sit alone on your little island and you need help ... who are you going to call? If you can't think of anyone, then how can you make things happen? How can you change the world? How can you change your world?

Who you know is incredibly important. Building your network doesn't have to be hard. It just has to be. So start building it.

Power Is Who You Know

QUESTIONS TO CONSIDER

- How can connections give you power?

  _____

  _____

  _____

  What are some ways you can network or connect with others?

  _____

  _____

  _____

- What's your elevator pitch?

  _____

  _____

  _____

ACTIONS TO CONSIDER

Connect with my neighborhood. Make a list of places you go on a daily, weekly or monthly basis. Some examples can be school, church, library, work, recreation center, etc. Next to each place, write who and how you can make connections there. Then begin to make those connections and expand your network.

"Think twice before you speak, because your words and influence will plant the seed of either success or failure in the mind of another." – Napoleon Hill

POWER IS WHAT YOU SAY

The words you choose have power. I started my career with my mouth. With words. I didn't have money. I didn't have an inheritance. I was a poor kid from a poor neighborhood who had a voice. I didn't have some cool invention to make me money. But I had a voice and with that voice, I changed my life. And my world.

I don't just say that ... I mean it. Your words can give you power. Or they can take it away.

There is power in what you say and who you say it to. Everything begins with the words you choose.

Ask not what your country can do for you ... ask what you can do for your country – John F. Kennedy

I regret that I have but one life to lose for my country – Nathan Hale

Darkness cannot drive out darkness; only light can do that. Hate cannot drive out hate; only love can do that – Dr. Martin Luther King, Jr.

Each of these quotes has resonated through people, cultures, societies, and through the years. Nathan Hale was 21 in 1776 when he was captured by the British Army and uttered those words as the noose was placed around his neck. It was the first time anyone had referred to the American Colonies as a country. His words spread like wildfire throughout the thirteen colonies and inspired more men to fight for freedom.

Words matter.

The Words

When I was kid, I would get pulled out of class for speech pathology sessions. I slurred a little when I spoke (a foreshadowing of my hearing impairment.) There was an exercise that I enjoyed playing with the other students that would be in the session with me.

Basically, the therapist would show us a word and then we would have to describe that word with another word. No word could be used twice. The way I looked at it, you had two strategies to choose from. First, you can look for simple, common words and hope that you chose that word before someone else could use it, or you can find a word that no one else will use. The ones who would win this little game are usually the ones that choose to be patient and find a more articulate word. I always chose to find the more articulate word.

In order for words to be powerful for you, you have to gain a good grasp on vocabulary.

Today, swearing is so common among younger generations that they're almost a part of the vernacular (look that word up ... use the tools that surround you to grow your knowledge!). It may be cool or funny from time to time and it may even get a reaction out of people, but overall it's a crutch. It's a handicap that people tend to use when they don't have a strong vocabulary (but that's not always the case, but often).

You don't want words to master you. Then you don't have power. You want to become a master of words.

I was called garbage when I was a kid. I was told I wouldn't amount to anything. What those people (some of them teachers) didn't know was that I read all of the time. I read comic books. When I didn't have any more, I read books.

As I got older, I wanted to rap, or be a DJ, and I knew the best way to be good at that was to build my vocabulary, so I even started reading the dictionary. Real exciting, right?

Maybe not, but you know what? I had some pretty good words to choose from when I needed to. When you have a good grasp of language and you have a sharp mind, and if you're a smart-ass like I was, it can get you into trouble. I had an English teacher in high school who once wrote down on an essay I had submitted that my writing was 'nonsensical.' I stared at that word and didn't have a clue what it meant. I went home, looked it up, and said to myself, 'that b****!' I felt powerless in that moment. From then on, I wanted to know what words meant.

My strength of vocabulary certainly got me into trouble from time to time. Absolutely. But I learned that I could use my words to tear someone down ... or build them up.

Martin Luther King, Jr. always fascinated me. His use of language was powerful. He could say something immensely meaningful and powerful and do so while keeping it simple so that everyone could understand.

If you want to be powerful, you need to improve your language. That doesn't mean you're going to have to walk around talking like some dystopian troglodyte with a cantankerous attitude and blithe smile. (yeah, I had to look all that up to write it.)

But when you build a stronger vocabulary, you suddenly have more ammunition in your personal arsenal to help you understand when people are expecting to put you in a corner or label you and you can add dimension to the things you want to say.

Try this: come up with a six word statement that defines you. Sounds easy at first, doesn't it? But it's not that easy to get down to six words the meaning of you.

Mine is 'P*assionate, creative force for positive change.*'

Find your six words. You'll struggle with it, but it's worth the effort. Trust me.

But once you find the words. Once you master the words. Those words will make you powerful.

The Conversation

Communication is crucial. You need to be able to communicate with people. There's talking and then there's communicating and they're not one in the same. You have to make sure that the meaning of the words you're saying are being understood in the manner that you meant them to be understood.

Let me rephrase that.

How you mean something isn't always how it will be understood. Most disagreements, conflicts, and misunderstandings come from poor communication. If my wife comes up to me and says, 'How does this look?' about a dress she's wearing, I might say, 'It looks okay.'

Harmless, right? Uh-uh. That simple statement could put me in the doghouse for a week! There's tone, body language, inflection, and eye contact that all matter. When a woman asks how she looks, 'okay' to her might sound like, 'not good,' 'ugly,' 'I've seen you look better,' or any number of other things.

There's a difference between communication and effective communication. It matters how you communicate, it matters how you hold a conversation.

Always test for comprehension. Make sure people understand what you're saying. Are people looking away? Are they fidgeting? Do they look disconnected? Disinterested? If so, then you're not connecting. You're not holding the conversation and you're losing power.

When I was growing up, my father would come home on Friday nights, knowing my mother didn't cook on Friday or Saturday nights, and he would ask, 'Baby, what do you want to eat for dinner?'

Now, my father was the typical hunter/gatherer. He wanted to know what to get, then he'd go out and get it. If she wanted moose, he'd go find a moose, kill it, and bring it home. My mother, on the other hand, saw the question as dialogue. So she would say, 'I don't know baby, what do you want?' The fight started shortly thereafter and I would end up ordering a pizza for my sisters and me.

Many years later, I was married with children of my own and I called my wife and asked her, 'Baby, what do you want to eat for dinner?' She replied, 'I don't know baby, what do you want to eat for dinner?' and I started having flashbacks and suddenly hated pizza.

I knew I had to communicate effectively in order for her to understand me. I couldn't place my history on her; otherwise I'd end up repeating my parent's ill-fated Friday night conversations. So I took a breath and then responded, 'You're a complicated person with many likes and dislikes, specific tastes, and I will eat anything, as you know, and because I'm a hunter/gatherer, like my father before me, who will go out and kill a moose (okay, I'd probably go to a store that sold moose) if that's what you want, I would prefer you tell me what you would like to eat tonight.'

She told me she wanted sushi and the problem was solved. Communication. Effective communication. You have to have conversations. It's all about the conversations.

In order to do it right, you have to bring all of your powers to bear. Your knowledge, the look and feel, what you say, how you say it ... everything. Use your words in effective conversations with the individuals in your life and you will gain power.

The Solo

So what about speaking in public? Just got a shiver through your body, did you? More people fear speaking in public than dying. That means that most people would rather be the person in the casket than the person giving the eulogy.

Obviously, for me speaking in public is not a fear. The trick is that I don't think about it as speaking in front of 500 people. I think about it as having 500 conversations with 500 different people.

To have the confidence to speak in public requires practice and your voice. Practice can be done in front of a mirror, friends, family, and building from there. But there's no escape from practice. You either do it or you don't.

Your voice is built upon two foundations. Your message, or what you want to say, and your purpose, why you want to say it.

Your message has to be clear. What is it that you want to say? What is it you want people to understand?

To know? To think? To feel? Your purpose (the why) also needs to be clear. Why do you want them to understand, to know, to think, to feel?

Your message and your purpose make up your voice. One you have that, you just have to figure out *how* you want to say it. Tell stories. Tell facts about yourself. Tell facts about others. Use PowerPoint. Use a flipchart. If you don't do well behind a podium, step out from behind it. Find what works best for you, not what works best for others. Find your own style. Find the way that allows you to communicate most comfortably and effectively as possible. But no matter what style you choose, always, always, always, always speak from the heart.

Once you are able to find your voice and how you want to share it then begin to work out your solo. Get an opening statement, drop in your message, add in the purpose of your message, and give supporting evidence for your message, then close strong. That's how you build a solo.

Many students I talk to don't think they're very good at the solo. Mostly because they never tried. I had one girl who thought that she wasn't very good at all and she got up and said, nervously, mind you, *"My name is (so-and-so). I want to stop bullying in my school because so many people kill themselves because of bullying and I've been bullied."*

As she spoke, I thought, 'This is good.' That was her opening statement, her message and her purpose. It was a good start. All she needed to do next was drop facts, and she said, *"One out of every four kids is bullied every year. 1 in 4! That's 25% of you. That means that when you walk down the halls next time, count off every fourth person you pass and see how many are victims of bullying.* Now, she needed to make the personal connection, speak from the heart and bring it home. Then she did it. *"I'm so and so and I'm the power of youth and I want to stop bullying."*

Boom. Bam. Done. Yes! She nailed it. You can too. It's your solo. It's easy when you know what you're saying and why you're saying it. You have to believe in it.

When you have the words, you can have meaningful, effective conversations and deliver powerful solos, which give way to your directive.

The Directive

Your directive is a verbal representation of your power. It involves everything we've talked about in this book. It's who you are, your purpose, what you believe, what you know, what you do, what you value. It's everything, your words, your passion, and your manifesto. Your directive is the communication you share with the world, so they know who you are, what you are about and what you plan to use your power to change.

My directive is simple. Every child should be empowered to make their dreams a reality, manifest their destiny and realize their full potential. Ensuring that ensures our future and cements our legacy. Where did that come from? From the way some of my teachers treated me. From having so many of my peers end up on the wrong side of success.

From losing my godson at such an early age, never being able to live a full life. From seeing firsthand the power of education and what it has done to change my life and the life of my family. All of these experiences and so many more shaped and molded my directive. And my directive is a representation of my power. Who I am, my purpose, my beliefs, my values, my knowledge; all of it. It's why I speak, it's why I wrote this book and it's how I live my life.

So, what's your directive? What is the verbal representation of your power? What is it you want to change? Do you want to end gang violence? Do you want to stop bullying? Do you want to end abuse? Do you want to empower more youth?

Every student has a directive within them that they want to share. What's yours?

Your words, the conversation, and the solo all come together to create your directive. Record it, take it to school board, and stake your claim. Let the world hear it, know it and feel it. Your voice is your power. My voice is my power. Our voices are our power. Let them be heard.

Power Is What You Say

QUESTIONS TO CONSIDER

- How can words get you in trouble?

  _____

  _____

- How can words build people up?

  _____

  _____

- Do you enjoy speaking publicly? If not, how can you make it easier?

  _____

  _____

ACTIONS TO CONSIDER

Me in 6. Words matter. They are important and they can be deeply meaningful. Come up with a six word statement that defines you, that describes who you are and want to be. For example, mine would be: 'Passionate, creative force for positive change.' Choose your words wisely. Then, write it down, share with your friends and family, post it on your social media, and let everyone know your words.

"Think twice before you speak, because your words and influence will plant the seed of either success or failure in the mind of another." – Napoleon Hill

POWER IS HOW YOU USE IT

Back in the first paragraph, I posed the question to you: *what is power?*

It's an interesting question with many possible answers, depending on whom you speak to about it. I want you to try and recall what you were thinking about when you first read that question.

What is power?

What came into your mind? Was it an idea? An image of a person you might consider powerful? Or was it something like a machine, a nice racing car, or a hard hit in football?

Even though we often attach labels of 'good' and 'bad' to symbols of power, such as Hitler being possessed of bad power, or Martin Luther King, Jr. as having possessed good power, the labels don't attach themselves to the power itself, but rather to the individuals who wielded that power and how they *chose* to use it.

Power is neutral. It's neither good nor bad. It simply *is*.

Power is defined by what you do and how you use it. It is said that influential people are powerful, but there are plenty of powerful people who aren't influential.

You have power within you. It may be dormant, it may be sitting there without your knowledge, but it's there. You need to cultivate that power. You need to transform it into influence. How do you do that?

By using that power to help others.

Sure, you could use your power to simply earn money, to get things for yourself, but what's the point? You surround yourself with material possessions, a nice house, fancy cars, and fake people all telling you what you want to hear but no one telling you what you *need* to hear and what do you have?

An empty life to look back upon and all those people whom you thought were friends will be gone the minute the money runs out. Just ask MC Hammer. Hammer had the pop hit 'Hammer Time' in the 1990s and was a mega star for a while. He made millions of dollars and he brought along an entourage of people with him everywhere he went. People who had been there before he was a big star, but when his money dried up, so did they. He might have been trying to help those people by giving them jobs they didn't deserve or do anything to earn, but it was misplaced sentiment. He didn't have any real power.

When you use your power to help others in meaningful ways (not buying them things), then you multiply your power.

Build your knowledge base. Increase your network power. Develop who you are and when you need someone, they'll be there for you. By doing this, you increase your power tenfold.

True power is about service. Service to others. To family, to friends, to your community, to your country, to this world.

In order to truly cultivate power, you have to leave the world around you better than you found it. My father taught me that a long time ago. It's about leaving your mark. Leaving your legacy.

Let's fast forward into the future to your final days. Looking back, how do you think you will be remembered? How do you want to be remembered? If you could write your own epitaph (an epitaph is a short text honoring someone who has passed away) what would it say? What would you want yours to say? What mark do you want to leave behind?

Yeah, Jose could really take it to the hoop. Man, Marco could rap like da bomb. Mary got straight Cs.

Are those powerful? Is that going to leave a lasting impression? Would something like that be enough for you if today was your last day?

I don't believe that. You shouldn't accept that. That's not enough, not when you have power.

When I was a kid, I had insomnia. My brain would be going a hundred miles an hour when I laid down to sleep. Whenever I *did* manage to sleep, I had nightmares. You know, the kind where you wake up frightened to death but not sure what scared you so much. I'd wake up, my brain would get going, and that would be it. Game over.

Over time, I learned to cope with it. The insomnia eventually subsided. I started sleeping like a normal human being. When I landed a job as a grad assistant, earning my MBA, and ready to join corporate America and make the big bucks, I was told that I was deaf. I had a hearing impairment. I was, to be honest, thrown off my game. I didn't know what to make of it.

That was about the same time I started to get close to Anthony, a cousin of mine. He was from a different family and we were related through my grandfather, Anthony lived in Lawrence, Massachusetts, outside of Boston.

Well, it turned out that my hearing impairment was hereditary. My cousin Anthony had been born with no ears. He went through a number of reconstructive surgeries to build them and he had cochlear implants so he could hear. He looked sort of normal, but also sort of not normal. As you probably well know, kids can be cruel, harsh, and even evil at times. I expected Anthony would have had a rough time in school.

But I was wrong. He had a good life. Kids loved him. He was part of a dance group, even! He'd be up front dancing his heart out. He had a beautiful girlfriend. He impacted lives.

He and I started to communicate by email and instant messages. He put things in perspective for me. He calmed me down about my hearing impairment. I realized that I needed to stop complaining and worrying. I needed to stop feeling sorry for myself. We talked all the time. When my son was born, Anthony wanted to come down and meet him. So they did, on Memorial Day weekend. We had a great time, he taught me how to dance and I pretty much showed him how *not* to dance.

As the day wore on, we had an amazing day, but the baby was getting tired and irritable. So my wife and I said our goodbyes and returned home.

We arrived to a ringing phone. It was my mother. She told me I had to get to Lehigh Valley Hospital right away. I raced out and when I arrived, I watched a trauma helicopter landing and something in my gut told me that I was connected to whoever was in that chopper. I found my family and they recounted the story.

Anthony and his family were returning to their hotel shortly after I left. They were turning into the parking lot when two guys were drag racing down the street. One of them swerved and missed Anthony and his family. The other one t-boned them. Anthony was killed on impact. His mother was in critical condition. She was the one in the helicopter.

I greeted my uncle and he had blood on his shirt, so I gave him mine. When the doctor asked the family to come in the other room, I wouldn't go. I knew what he would tell them. The shrieks and sobs confirmed what I already knew.

We didn't tell Anthony's mother right away, but she pulled through.

When my family traveled to Boston for the funeral, we did so in six cars. When we arrived, I couldn't believe what I saw. The viewing had hundreds of people. There were all types of people, Black, White, tall, short, fat, young, and old. There were so many people and a line that never quit. All for a 14 year old.

Anthony impacted lives.

The procession was inspiring, amazing. The cathedral was packed. The priest wore a Yankees baseball cap (in Red Sox country, mind you) because that was Anthony's favorite team. I sat there and listened as the priest read a letter that Anthony once wrote. It was a letter about a mentor, someone he looked up to. The priest finished the letter then looked at me and told me I was that mentor.

Me, Chu, the one with the mouth, who always had something to say ... was speechless.

Me? Anthony looked up to *me*? No, no, no. The kid had it all wrong. He was *my* hero! He was unselfish, unwavering, loyal, and optimistic. How could *I* be *his* hero?

I returned home and immediately had trouble sleeping. The nightmares had returned. I'd wake up with my heart racing, but not remembering the dream. Until finally one night I did.

I was walking alone along a deserted beach. I was naked (sorry to put that image in your head), and I stepped into the water. I just kept walking, feeling the sand beneath my feet and the water rolling up and down over my body as I got deeper and deeper. When I realized that I was going too far, I turned back and struggled to get back to the shore.

I saw my footprints as the tide kept pulling me back out. Then I watched as those footprints slowly were being erased by wave after wave after wave.

The water was erasing all evidence that I ever existed. I realized in that moment that I was scared of dying before making any significant contribution to this world.

I had to stop leaving footprints in the sand. I had to leave them in stone. So that not only would people know that this is where I claimed my legacy, where I stood my ground, where I used my voice, where I left my mark, my legacy. And they would be able to follow my footsteps and take them farther. My cousin Anthony didn't leave footprints in the sand. He left them in stone. I needed to do the same.

At the end of the day, true power is about true service.

Rudy Giuliani was a powerful mayor of New York City. He transformed the city. But if you ask people what they most remember him for, whether it was for cleaning up Times Square, removing all the homeless people in Manhattan, or after 9/11 when he dedicated his life to helping people the most, most will claim the latter.

It is in the moment when we help each other, when we're vulnerable, when we are out there sacrificing, when we're most powerful.

When you use your power to help others, your power will grow.

Here's my challenge to you right now ... Sit down and think about what you'll do with your power. What changes will you make in your life and for those around you? In your school? In your family? In your community?

Will you leave footprints in the sand? Or will you leave your mark in stone so that people will follow you? Will you use your voice? Will you use your power?

Because the power of youth is within you. It all begins with you. The Power of Youth is YOU! Now use it to change the world.

Power Is How You Use It

Questions to Consider

- How can you use your power to help others?

  _____

  _____

- What do you want your legacy to be?

  _____

  _____

- What changes can you make in your life to utilize your power?

  _____

  _____

Actions To Consider

Give a little bit. You have been given $5,000, but you cannot use it on yourself. Write a detailed explanation of who and how you would spend it. After that, think of ways that you could give to the people and causes you outlined now. You can give your attention, your affection, or your time. You could prepare a slideshow presentation or video to showcase a cause, hold a volunteer fair where different volunteer organizations or opportunities are outlined and other students have a chance to join in or simply donate $5. Do anything and everything you can now. Give a little bit and change a whole lot.

Made in the USA
Monee, IL
13 August 2022

10967519R00075